DICTIONARY OF STITCHES

DICTIONARY OF STITCHES

Edited by
Sheila Brull

CAVENDISH HOUSE

Published by Marshall Cavendish Books Limited
58 Old Compton Street, London W1V 5PA

© Marshall Cavendish Limited 1976-84

ISBN 0 85685 130 2

Printed and bound in Hong Kong by
Dai Nippon Printing Company Limited

HOW TO USE THIS BOOK

The Dictionary of Stitches is a full and useful reference to many different techniques. Included in the alphabetical list of embroidery and sewing methods there are detailed descriptions of many allied techniques such as patchwork, smocking and canvas work. You might want to try your hand at macramé, needle-made lace or tatting, or simply discover an exciting new knitting or crochet stitch. A comprehensive index has been included, designed to help you find your way around easily, and this has been carefully cross-referenced. A knitted pocket, for example, would be described both under the headings of 'Pockets' and 'Knitting'. You will find the index on page 213.

Our intention is to help you add a new dimension of variety to your stitchcraft. Take canvas work, for instance. Why stick to conventional half cross stitch when there are about 20 other variations to try, all listed under the main 'Canvas work' heading. Have you heard of Tunisian or hairpin crochet? Do you know how to do Italian quilting? You can find all the answers under the appropriate entries and more inspiration from the many beautiful illustrations. Besides all this, the other aspects of plain sewing and mending have not been neglected and these will provide a great deal of help for the busy and budget-conscious needle woman. You can be practical with patching, grafting and darning, individual with monograms or glamorous with beading and gold embroidery. Just turn the pages of this book and you will see that it contains instructions for them all.

Antique or tuscan

A traditional Italian style of embroidery on evenly-woven white or unbleached fabric. It is carried out in a similar way to counted thread work using either pale or natural coloured yarn and satin, overcast, four-sided and clustered hem stitches.

Appliqué

The technique of applying one fabric to decorate another. Methods of working depend on the fabrics used. Firm, non-fraying materials can be cut to shape, slipstitched by hand or zigzag stitched with a swing needle sewing machine. Thin fabrics that are likely to fray should be cut larger than needed, then the exact shape closely buttonhole stitched or zigzag stitched all round and the surplus fabric

This simple spray of apple blossom makes a charming motif for appliqué work. You can trace the life-size design from this page.

7

The Zodiac sign Pisces inspired these formalized fish worked in hemmed applique and then decorated with various embroidery stitches.

trimmed off close to stitching. Another method for thin fabrics is to tack down a small hem all round and slipstitch into place. Embroidery such as Bermuda faggoting, Paris or Turkish stitches can be used for strong yet decorative application. Example illustrated on page 7 is American patchwork which is closer to appliqué in spite of its name and traditionally used for bed covers.

Arezzo

In contrast with Assisi embroidery work where the motif is left un-worked but is silhouetted with cross stitch, these motifs are embroidered and the background left plain. The fabric used need not have an even weave, it can be either natural or coloured to tone with the blue or rust yarn of the embroidery. Motifs are filled with a type of Slav stitch with outlines in drawn fabric and hems in four-sided stitch.

Arrowheads

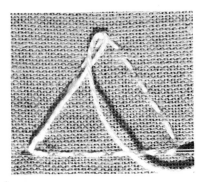

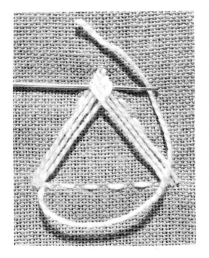

Used to finish off ends of pleats or bound pockets. With chalk, mark a triangle the required size, then mark outline with a small running stitch. Using silk buttonhole twist start at the bottom left hand corner, take needle up to top and bring it through to pick up a small stitch (1). Next take needle to bottom right hand corner, passing it through underneath and out at left. Continue, laying each thread inside the previous one (2) placing stitches side by side and gradually filling the triangle.

Ars canusina

A traditional Italian embroidery style, worked with or without a frame. Motifs consist of fine drawn thread work outlined with

stem stitch which is worked right round the motif then back again to form a bold border.

Assisi embroidery

This is worked by the counted thread and therefore an even weave fabric in either cotton or linen must be used. Designs are usually worked in two colours, either blue or rust for the cross stitch background and black or some other strongly contrasting colour for the Holbein stitch outlines. The actual motif is left in the plain background fabric. Both Holbein and cross stitches must be worked over the same number of threads using stranded cotton, soft embroidery cotton, pearl cotton or *coton à broder*.

B

Mythical creatures are typical of those depicted in traditional Assisi embroidery. The outline and details are defined in double running or Holbein stitch and the background is filled in with solid areas of cross stitch. This design has been worked over four threads each way on even-weave linen in shades of pearl cotton.

Back stitch

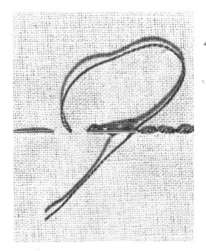

Bring needle through to right side of fabric and make a small stitch backwards. Then bring needle through again a little in front of the first stitch and take another back stitch to the front of the first stitch. Continue, working from right to left.

Back stitch, doubled

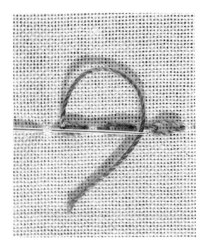

Make a stitch backwards as for back stitch. Then, instead of bringing needle through again in front of this stitch, bring it through where you started and do the stitch over again. Continue as for back stitch, working each stitch twice over.

Back stitch, half

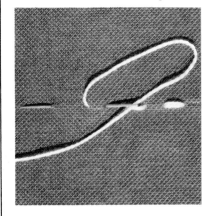

This simple variation is one that can be used equally effectively as a decorative line stitch for embroidery or as a practical, hard wearing seam in hand sewing. Work as for back stitch but take each stitch over three threads of fabric leaving a three-thread space between each stitch. Use for any seam or join where strength is required.

Bandera

Typical Italian embroidery of the 17th and 18th centuries. The designs were rich with birds, flowers and fruit, worked on coarse linen in stem stitch, Bokhara couching and split stitch in beautifully shaded yarns.

Bars

These bars are used to strengthen cut-work, Hardanger and drawn-thread embroidery.

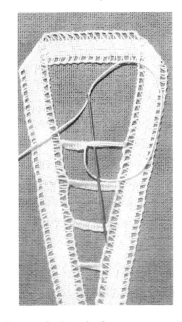

Buttonhole stitch
Throw three long threads across the gap to be bridged. Work buttonhole stitch closely over these threads.

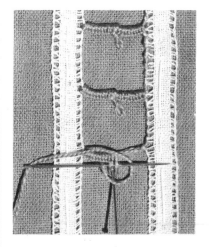

With picot
Work buttonhole stitch until half-way across bar. When forming next stitch, pull top loop upwards, hold with pin, take needle underneath and continue buttonhole stitching. When loop is secure remove pin.

11

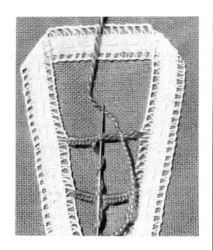

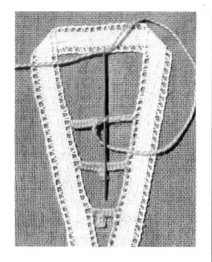

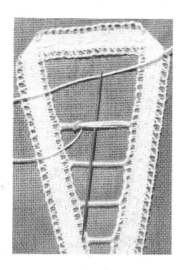

With bullion knot

This variation shows how two embroidery stitches can be combined to produce an interesting effect. Work buttonhole stitch half-way across bar. On next stitch twist thread several times round the needle and insert needle back into last buttonhole stitch. Continue to end.

With loops

These are frequently used when working Renaissance lace. Work buttonhole stitch to half way across foundation threads, then re-insert needle into last stitch and work two or three little loops. Continue buttonhole stitch to end of bar. The size of these loops and the number used are a matter of taste and depend on the character of the work.

Overcast bar

Prepare as for buttonhole stitch bar but cover foundation threads with closely worked overcasting.

Beading

Use fine, strong cotton or silk thread in a colour suited to both background fabric and beads. Before use, draw thread once across beeswax and use double thickness. Beading needles are long and fine (sizes 10 to 13) and a frame is generally advisable.

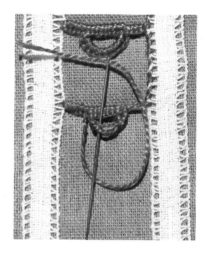

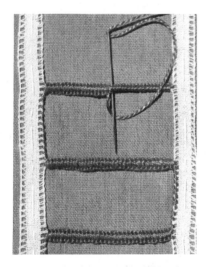

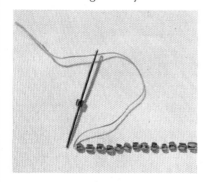

With buttonhole ring

Work buttonhole stitch to two-thirds of the way across the foundation threads, then take thread back far enough to make a semi-circular loop when covered with buttonhole stitch. Do this twice more to form foundation for ring, cover with buttonhole stitch and continue to end of bar.

Grape motif in tambour beading using metallic sequins and gold bugle beads.

Double buttonhole stitch

Prepare as for buttonhole stitch bar but work the buttonhole stitching loosely. Turn work and make a second row of buttonhole stitching between the stitches of the previous row. This type of bar can be used in drawn-thread work when the foundation is formed by the threads of the fabric.

Beads stitched down separately

Bring needle through to front of work and pick up one bead. Slide it along the needle and just on to the thread. Pick up one thread of background fabric, the length of the bead along the design line. Draw needle through fabric to place bead on fabric and pick up second bead.

B

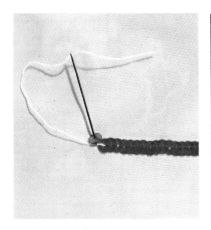

Scale effect
Bring needle up through the hole of the sequin, set sequin on fabric and take a tiny stitch to the side of it on the line of the design. Bring needle up through next sequin and continue to end of line. This results in a scale-like effect and can be used for working larger solid areas of beading. Variations can be produced by using sequins in contrasting colours.

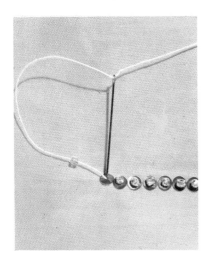

Sequin held with small bead
Each sequin is held in place by a small bead which must be larger than the hole in the sequin. Bring needle up through hole, pick up a bead on needle and insert needle back through hole in sequin. Bring needle up through hole in next sequin and continue to end of line. Beads can either match or contrast with sequins.

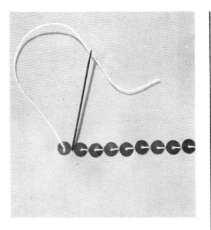

Single back stitch
Each sequin is sewn to the fabric with a single back stitch, a contrasting thread may be used. The tension of the stitches should be firm but not too tight. Make sure that the thread is fastened off securely at both ends of a row of beads.

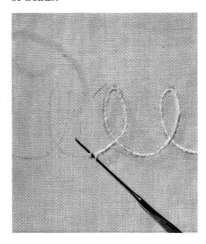

Tambour beading
Beads and sequins are attached by means of a small sharp hook in a holder. This is used in the same way as a crochet hook to make chain stitches through the fabric. Mark design to be worked on wrong side of fabric and place in frame. Thread beads on to a spool of cotton (in pattern sequence if required). Hold hook in right hand above frame, the left hand holding the thread and flick up a bead beyond the hook as each stitch is made. For a speckled effect, flick up a bead for every second stitch.

Bermuda faggoting

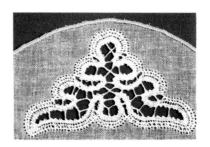

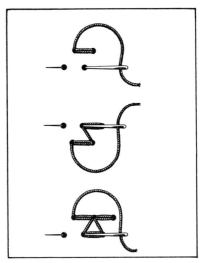

This name is only used when the stitch holds down a small hem on fine fabric, or covers the join when one fine fabric is applied to another. Work from right to left as shown in the diagrams.

Binding

With bias strip
To find the true bias, fold a square of fabric so that the warp and weft threads coincide exactly. Cut through resulting fold. Width of strips should be four times finished width of binding and length as required. Pin and tack bias strips to garment, right sides together, raw edges level, with stitching line one quarter of width of bias from edge, matching fitting line on garment. Stitch binding to garment, remove tack-

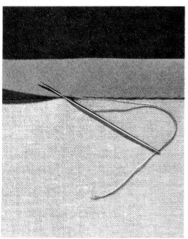

ing and trim edges level. Fold under raw edge of binding. Bring fold over raw edge to stitching line on garment, pin and tack so that binding is quite even on either side and hem lightly by hand as shown in the illustration. Commercial bias binding is applied in exactly the same way.

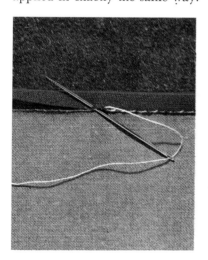

With braid

Side of braid which will be uppermost should be stitched first. With right sides together, pin braid about 3mm ($\frac{1}{8}$in) from edge, leaving about 1cm ($\frac{3}{8}$in) extending to neaten afterwards. Stitch braid into place. Turn braid over raw edge and cover stitching line on underside with edge of braid. Hem lightly by hand. Another method is to fold braid exactly in half over edge of garment and machine stitch in place.

Bobbin lace

The bobbins are wooden rods with small heads at one end. Thread is wound round the bobbin so that it acts as a spool and also weights the thread. A lace pillow is used as a base on which to work and is usually cylindrical, about 36cm (14in) long and 18cm (7in) in diameter. It is usually filled with straw or sand and covered with fine linen or cotton in a light colour. Thread used does not necessarily have to be very fine, but must be strong and twisted. Lace pins are used to hold patterns in shape until completed. Brass or brass plated pins are best. Patterns are marked out on a pricking card and worked over it. This card can be bought by the sheet and holes made in it where the pins will be placed with a pricker or punch.

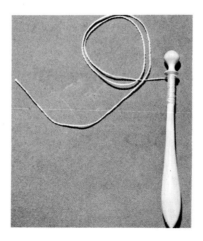

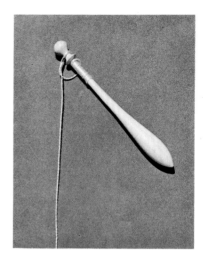

Winding the bobbins

The lace is made by intertwining threads previously wound on to bobbins. It is worked from a chart which is firmly fixed to the pillow.

Wind thread round narrowest part of bobbin. Holding bobbin in right hand, arrange end of thread in a double loop by winding it twice round first two fingers of left hand (1). Insert head of bobbin into loop. Hold loop in place with index finger of right hand and pull end of thread with left hand. Continue to ease thread through until knot is in place (2).

Basic movements

For basic lacemaking a set of four bobbins is required, one pair for each hand. Tie the four threads in pairs, making sure knot is secure. Fix threads to lace pillow with lace pins, either between the threads or through knot itself. If you were following a pattern, threads would be fixed to a chart at this stage. Length of thread between bobbin and lace should be about 15cm (6in) otherwise threads can easily become tangled. Lace making is difficult at first and you must be prepared for a lot of patient practice until you have mastered the basic stages and can work them automatically, but there can be fewer more fascinating and beautiful crafts.

B

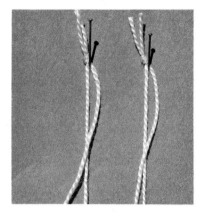

Stage one: turning This term describes the movement of passing the right bobbin over the left one.

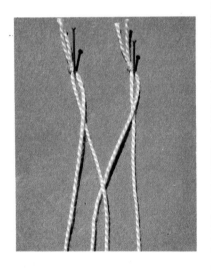

Stage two: crossing Where there are four bobbins, cross the inside bobbin of the left pair over the inside bobbin of the right pair. The outside bobbins are not moved.

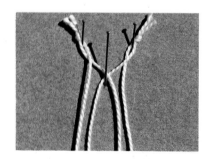

Half stitch
Turn both pairs of threads and then cross the centre threads. Fix the half stitch in place with a pin.

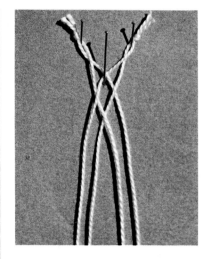

Full stitch
This is made by working a turning and a crossing immediately followed by another turning and crossing. The left pair of bobbins have now been transferred to the right side and the right pair to the left.

Forming braid
A close braid is made by working several full stitches consecutively.

Filet work foundation stitch
For square pieces of lace, borders and festoons, this stitch makes up the main motifs of the pattern. Motifs are linked by an openwork background. Copy the chart on to a piece of card or lacemaking parchment and pin it securely to the pillow. Fix a pair of bobbins to each of the points a, b, c, d, e.

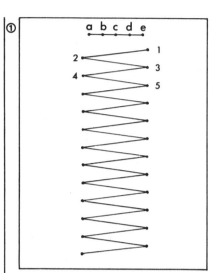

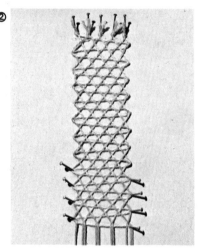

Turn the 1st and 2nd pairs of bobbins and cross. *Turn the 2nd and 3rd pairs and cross, repeat with the 3rd and 4th pairs and then with the 4th and 5th pairs. Turn the 5th pair of bobbins out at the right of the work and fix with a pin at point 1 on the chart. Turn the 5th pair of bobbins twice and the 4th pair once and cross. Turn the 4th and 3rd pairs and cross, repeat with the 3rd and 2nd pairs and then the 2nd and 1st. Fix the crossing with a pin at point 2 on the chart. Turn the 1st pair of bobbins twice, 2nd pair once, and cross. Repeat from *.

Opposite page, above: the famous Maltese lace being made. Below: a bobbin lace pattern being worked on a pillow.

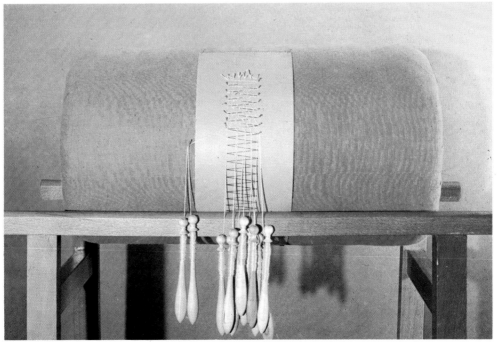

B

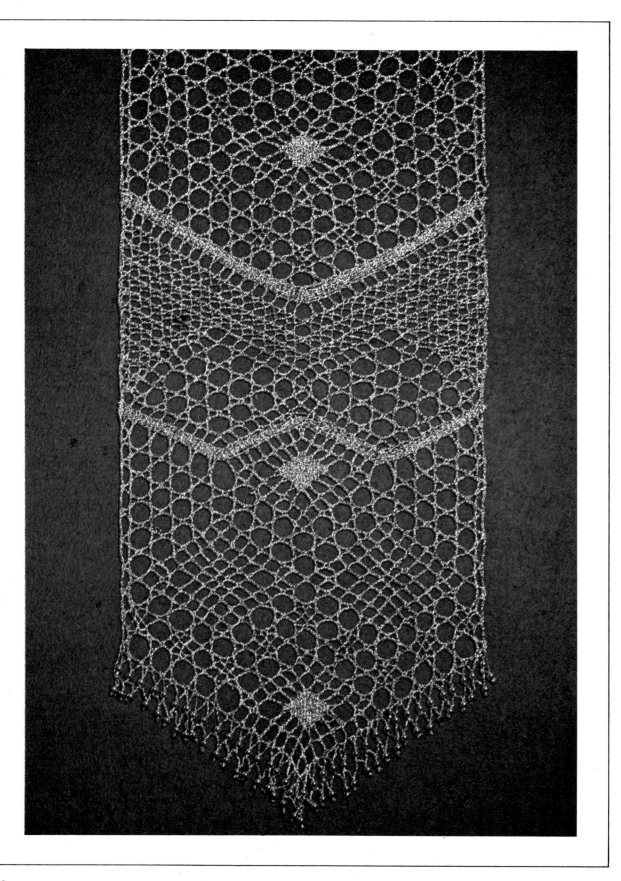

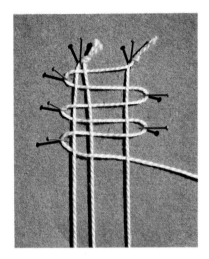

Herringbone background

Work this background on four bobbins. Using fourth bobbin, turn with the third bobbin, cross with the second, turn with the first one and pin. Still using the fourth thread, turn with the first bobbin, cross with the second, turn with the third and pin. In this way the fourth bobbin is passed from right to left and back again in a zigzag, weaving between the first three threads.

Weave foundation stitch

Weave stitch is a basic stitch which is used to make the main motifs of lace patterns. Nearly all weave stitches are made horizontally with the exception of some more complex stitches which are worked diagonally. Copy the chart on to a piece of card or lacemaking parchment and pin it firmly to the lace pillow. Place three pairs of bobbins to point a, two pairs to point b and two pairs to point c. * Cross the first two pairs of bobbins as if each pair were one thread. Then using the same four bobbins, make a half stitch. Cross the 2nd and 3rd pairs and make a half stitch. Cross the 3rd and 4th pairs and make a half stitch. Cross the 4th and 5th

Gold thread is used for this modern adaptation of bobbin lace to make a wall hanging trimmed with tiny beads.

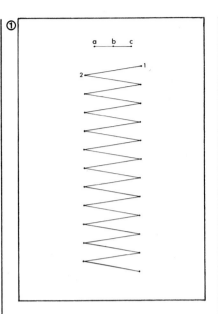

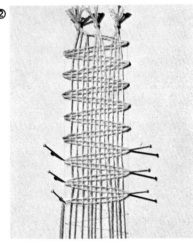

pairs and make a half stitch. Cross the 5th and 6th pairs and make a half stitch. Cross the 6th and 7th pairs and make a half stitch. Place a pin at point 1 on the chart and place the last pair of bobbins there. Turn this pair of bobbins and start working back. Cross the 7th and 6th pairs and make a half stitch. Cross the 6th and 5th pairs and make a half stitch. Cross the 5th and 4th pairs and make a half stitch. Cross the 4th and 3rd pairs and make a half stitch. Cross the 3rd and 2nd pairs and make a half stitch. Cross the 2nd and 1st pairs and make a half stitch. Fix the first pair of bobbins on a pin at point 2 on the chart, then turn them. Repeat from *.

Bokhara couching

Foundation thread being laid across the width of the design

Needle being brought out at edge of the design ready to lay the next thread

This stitch is useful and ornamental for filling in shapes of leaves and petals of flowers. It is worked in the same way as Rumanian stitch, but the small tying stitches are set at regular intervals over the laid thread (1) to form pattern lines across the shape. It should be worked in slanting lines with the laid thread fairly slack and the tying down stitches tight. (2) Avoid a tightly twisted thread which destroys the level surface but the direction of the lines can be varied.

Bokhara couching is used to embroider simple leaf motifs on table linen. This stitch is also useful for filling in backgrounds.

Braid

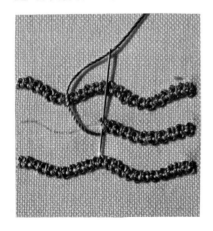

This is a kind of plaited ribbon used for binding. There are also grosgrain, petersham, embroidered cotton or wool braids. Some of the most exciting fancy braids can be found in furnishing trimming departments. Make sure at the time of purchase that the braid will not shrink. Use it to decorate clothes or furnishings. Types can vary from rich and decorative to those simple enough for children's wear. Apply by machine close to the edge or by hand using Paris or Turkish stitches, or Bermuda faggoting.

Braid stitch

This is most successfully worked in a thick unstranded thread. It should be compact and not too large and loose or the slightly raised effect will be lost. Work between two parallel guide lines. Start at lower right hand end and make a loop with the thread, holding it in place with left thumb. Insert needle through top line of border, bringing it out vertically on lower line. Pull loop tightly round needle, taking working thread under point from right to left. Pull thread through, ready for next stitch.

Broccatello

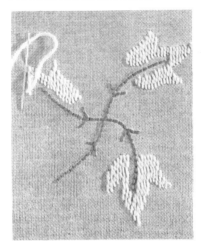

An Italian filling stitch similar to Bokhara couching. Each vertical stitch is tied with a small oblique stitch worked from left to right, so that the silhouette of the shapes that are filled appears to be irregular, formed of little parallel lines.

Broderie anglaise

This can be bought as a ready-made trimming in a variety of widths and patterns, double-sided, frilled or with slots for ribbon insertion. It is made of white cotton with embroidered eyelets. Attach by machine or by hand using Paris or Turkish

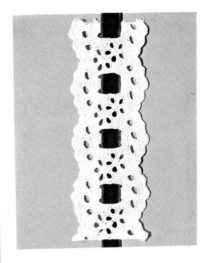

stitches or Bermuda faggoting. Broderie anglaise is a very popular trimming with a wide range of uses because it combines the decorative qualities of lace with the hard wearing properties of its cotton background.

Bulgarian embroidery

This border shows how even humble running stitch can be built up into rich motifs using pattern darning. The stitches of varying lengths are worked in rows to build up into a regular pattern. The thread is simply darned into the background fabric, keeping the tension even.

Braiding and self-fringing trim this set of linen table mats. Each
mat has four bands of braid in graduating tones of colour. The
braid is machine stitched into position and corners are mitred.

Bullion knot

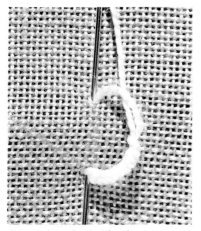

Completion of a bullion knot

Bullion knots worked in pairs

Make a back stitch the length of the knot required, but do not pull the needle right through the fabric. Twist the thread round the needle point as many times as needed to fill the length of the back stitch. Pull the needle through, holding the left thumb on the coiled thread. Then, still holding the coiled thread and twisting the needle back to where it was inserted, re-insert the needle in the same place. Pull the thread through until the bullion knot lies flat. Bullion knots worked in pairs as shown above can be used to form leaves or tiny flowers. Varying thicknesses of thread can be used to provide interesting textured effects.

Buttonholes

①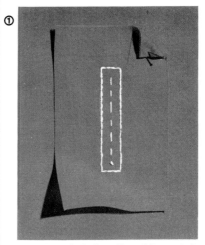

Machine stitched outline of buttonhole

②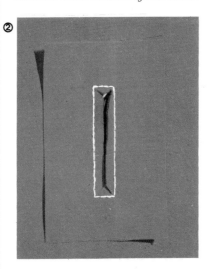

Cut down centre and into corners

③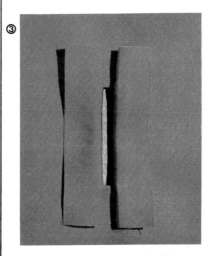

Binding pulled through to inside

④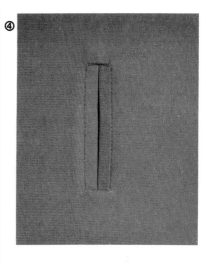

Bound

Measure out buttonhole position and mark. For each buttonhole cut a strip of fabric on the cross 5cm (2in) wide and 4cm (1½in) longer than buttonhole length. Working on outside of garment lay strip centrally over buttonhole position, right sides of fabric facing. Working on wrong side of fabric and using smallest stitch setting, stitch outline of buttonhole, shaping it into a perfect rectangle (1) running last stitches over first to secure.

Using sharp pointed scissors, cut into stitched area, taking care not to cut stitches at corners (2). Pull binding to inside (3). Press seam allowances away from opening. Turn work to outside and gently roll folded edges of binding so that they meet along centre of buttonhole with equal width to each side. Tack along opening. Turn work to inside and gently pull horizontal edges of binding fabric to make rolls continue evenly beyond opening of buttonhole (4). Catch them together. Press. Turn garment facing over buttonholes. Feel buttonhole through facing fabric and make a cut through facing to length of buttonhole opening. Turn in edges of cut and hem to buttonhole. If the ends of the cut are tight you must make the snip a little longer to take away the strain. A small bar can be stitched across each end to strengthen.

B

This rich design is of Bulgarian peasant origin and embroidered in
slanting Slav stitch, worked across two threads and up four on an
even-weave fabric. The black outlines are in back stitch and the
tiny squares are filled with four cross stitches. The vividness in
colour and boldness of the design suggest a dramatic wall panel.

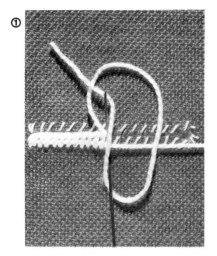

①

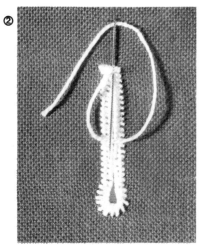

②

Worked (heavy fabric)
For very close weaves make the buttonholes with ordinary sewing thread. If fabric frays and grain is coarse use a heavier sewing thread or buttonhole twist. Mark length of buttonhole. Using sharp scissors, cut along the buttonhole length. Oversew cut edges with shallow stitches. Starting with a length of thread long enough to complete the buttonhole, work buttonhole stitches from left to right along its length. Insert needle into back of work and before pulling it through, bring thread from needle under point to form a loop. Pull forward into a small knot, placing it on the cut edge. Do not pull loops too tight or edge will roll. If stitches are worked too close together, the edge will cockle. For a padded effect, lay a thread along

line of buttonhole and work buttonhole stitch over this (1). Form a fan of stitches at the rounded end of the buttonhole, that is nearest front edge of garment, keeping the centre stitch in line with the slit (2). Turn the work and continue along top edge of buttonhole. Make a small bar across both rows of stitches at the end.

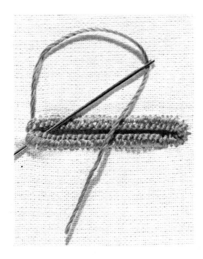

Worked (light fabric)
If garment is made in a fine fabric an underlay must be used to form another thickness. Neaten a small square of cotton and tack to wrong side of garment over slit before it is cut. (Check to be sure this does not show through on right side.) Work buttonholes with two rounded ends, then trim underlaid pieces as close as possible to buttonholes.

Buttonhole stitch embroidery

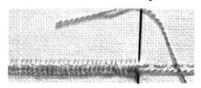

Worked from left to right. Bring needle out on lower line, then

insert the needle directly above and make a straight downward stitch, pulling the needle through over the working threads. This forms a row of straight stitches with a closely knotted edge on the lower line. For a padded effect, lay a thread along line to be stitched and work over this.

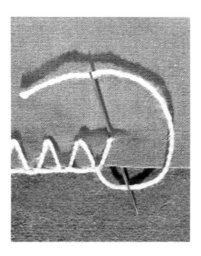

Closed
Similar to simple buttonhole stitch, but with the stitches worked in groups of two or three to form triangles.

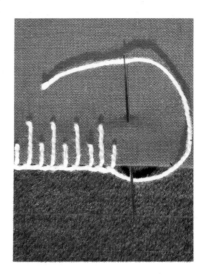

Long and short
A simple variation of buttonhole stitch worked according to personal taste. Useful for decorating household linen or applying motifs in appliqué work.

B

Widely spaced

The widely spaced form of buttonhole stitch is known as blanket stitch. It is a good strong stitch for sewing applied shapes.

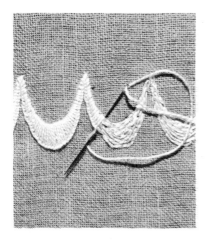

Padded

First outline shape to be worked with small running stitches, then fill with more running stitches and work buttonhole stitch over the padding. This is especially useful for strengthening scalloped edges.

Buttons

Rouleau shank

For buttons with large drill holes. Make a rouleau 3mm ($\frac{1}{8}$in) wide. Cut off a piece about 3.5cm ($1\frac{1}{4}$in) long and fill with buttonhole gimp (a cord-like thread mainly used by tailors). Thread through drill holes. To attach button, prize weave of garment open with stiletto or pointed end

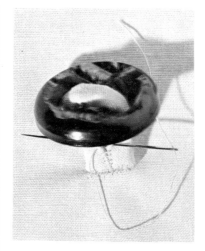

of knitting needle without breaking threads of fabric. Push ends of rouleau through hole to underside. Leave sufficient rouleau between button and garment to make a shank. Stitch down ends of rouleau inside garment, spreading them quite flat and catching ends of gimp into stitches so that it cannot work loose.

Stayed button

To reinforce buttons which receive extra strain or are sewn to a single thickness of fabric, place another smaller button or a small piece of tape directly underneath and sew together, through button, garment and reinforcing.

Thread shank

The length of a button shank should correspond with the thickness of the buttonhole. To make a

thread shank, place a matchstick or three pins across the button and make the stitches over them as you sew on the button. The matchstick lengthens the stitches and this makes the basis for the stem. Remove matchstick and twist the thread round the strands between button and garment. Finish off on wrong side with back stitches.

Byzantine embroidery

The motifs for this Italian embroidery are inspired by Byzantine mosaics. The backgrounds are completely filled with either split stitch or Bokhar a couching worked in either blue or rust, with figures left plain but outlined in black stem stitch.

Canvas work

To begin

Canvas used must be firm, supple and evenly woven. It can either be single or double thread depending on the thickness of thread to be used. Work in a slate frame, this helps to maintain correct shape (very small items need not be framed). To start, find centre of piece of canvas by folding it in half twice; mark centre lightly with a coloured crayon or thread. Start in the centre, do not use a knot, instead draw needle up through canvas, leaving a tail about 1.5cm (½in) long at back. Hold this thread close to canvas and work over it with the first few stitches. To finish off, darn thread into stitches at back of work to secure it. To continue with a new thread, darn its tail into back of previous row. When working a large area in one colour, use varying lengths of thread so that beginning and end of threads do not appear in line and cause a noticeable ridge.

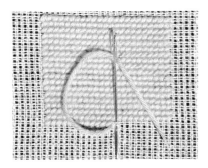

Half cross stitch

Work from left to right. Bring needle up through the canvas from bottom left, down through the next 'hole' on top right. This makes a diagonal stitch on the front and a short straight stitch on the back. Fasten off at the end of each patch of colour so that you do not leave long lengths of thread at the back.

Larger-than-life butterflies for a lovely panel worked in half cross stitch.

C

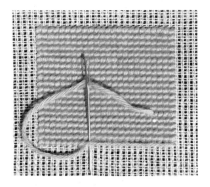

Half cross stitch over tramming

Tramming is a padding stitch which is used when the thread is not thick enough to cover the canvas completely. The tramming wool runs along each horizontal single canvas or pairs of threads called 'tramlines'. Bring the thread up through these tramlines, leaving a short tail at the back. Work in overlapping tramming stitches, not more than 13cm (5in) long, for the length of your working area. Then take the thread down through the tramlines again. Work the stitch over the tramming thread, binding in the tramming tails as you go.

This pretty trefoil design shows you how half cross stitch lends itself to small, neat patterns. If you make this up in a different combination of colours, the whole character of the design becomes more sophisticated. To add more

texture, you could work either the background or the trefoils in tiny cross stitch or tram the trefoils to give a raised effect.

Bricking

This upright stitch is worked in interlocking rows.
1st row Work alternate stitches over 4 horizontal threads.
2nd row Start 2 threads lower and work a row of stitches over 4 threads, between the stitches of the first row.

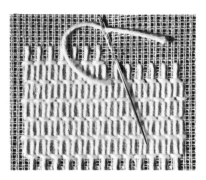

Bricking (Roman)

This gives a rich braiding effect. The stitch consists of two rows, linked with a row of horizontal stitches. Work from right to left, working each stitch from the top down over 6 threads, missing 1 hole between each stitch, then work the central cross bar over the stitch from left to right, 1 hole out on either side of the long stitch. The second row is worked in the same way, from right to left, but interlocking the stitches by bringing out the first stitch from the same hole as the crossing stitch of the previous row.

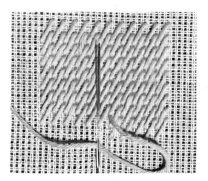

Bricking (slanted)

This stitch is also worked in interlocking rows, but over 4 vertical and 2 horizontal threads, which gives a smooth slanted texture.

Chain (method 1)

This is a very quick method worked with a fine crochet hook, missing 2 holes of the canvas with each stitch. For a shorter stitch miss 1 hole each time, for a longer one, miss more. Do not make the stitches too long or the work will wear badly. When one row is completed, finish off and start the next unless continuing in the same colour, in which case turn the work and commence the next row. It is essential to finish ends securely because if they work loose a whole row of stitching will come undone.

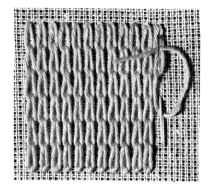

Chain (method 2)
Work this like ordinary chain stitch as shown in the illustration. Finish the end of each row with a small stitch to hold the last chain in place. Once again, finish off the end of the thread securely.

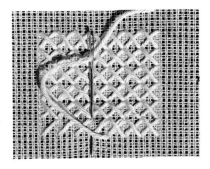

Cross stitch
Make a row of slanting stitches from left to right and then make another row from right to left on top of them. The picture shows the stitch worked with a thin wool so that you can see clearly how it builds up but of course, worked correctly, the canvas should be completely covered with yarn. Each cross stitch should add up to a perfect square and must always be worked over an equal number of threads, down and across. The upper stitches must always lie in the same direction. Despite its simplicity, cross stitch can be extremely effective.

Lakeside scene in bricking which gives faster coverage and more texture to the kind of design where half cross stitch is usually used. It is worked in two directions, with an occasional 'half brick' placed at angles where two colours or stitch directions meet.

C

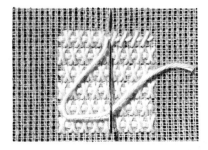

Cross (alternating)

This filling stitch is composed of two cross stitches of different sizes in interlocking rows. Work from right to left. Bring needle through 3rd hole down from top of work. Insert needle 1 hole up, 1 across. Bring needle through 2 holes down. Insert needle 3 holes up. 1 across. Bring needle through 2 holes down. Repeat to end of row. To complete the crosses work the return row from left to right. **Next row.** Bring needle through 4 holes down and work each row so that it interlocks with the one above by working the top of each stitch into the same holes as the bottom of the stitch above. This stitch would look effective worked in two contrasting colours.

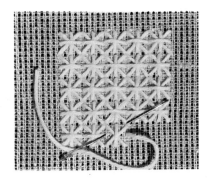

Cross (double)

In this stitch each star is completed before starting the next. To work one star bring the needle through at top left hand side of work. Insert needle 4 holes down, 4 across. Bring needle through 4 holes up. Insert needle 4 holes

A half cross stitch William Morris rose would make a pretty chair cover.

30

down, 4 back. Bring needle through 4 holes up, 2 across. Insert needle 4 holes down. Bring needle through 2 holes up, 2 back. Insert needle 4 holes across.

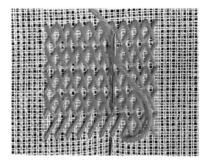

Cross (oblong)

Work in the same way as ordinary cross stitch but bring the needle through 5th hole down from the top of the work. Insert the needle 4 holes up, 2 across. Bring the needle through 4 holes down.

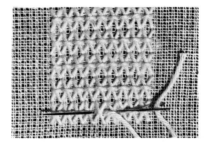

Cross (oblong with bars)

Begin by working oblong cross stitch, then work bars one row from right to left, the next row from left to right and so on. Bring needle through 3rd hole down, 3rd in from edge of work. Insert needle 2 holes back. Bring needle through 4 holes on. Repeat to end of row.

Cross (long-legged)

This differs from ordinary cross stitch only in that one of the crossing stitches is worked over twice as many threads as the other. Bring needle through 4th hole down from the top of work. Insert needle 8 holes across, 4 holes up. Bring needle through

4 holes down. Insert needle 4 holes up, 4 back. Bring needle through 4 holes down. Repeat to end of row.

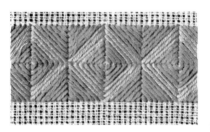

Cushion

Before working the plump squares of this stitch, decide which way the diagonal is going to lie, its direction will make quite a difference to the overall effect. To eliminate a gap between a group of 4 squares, make a diagonal tramming stitch from corner to corner of the whole block and work over this. Work each complete square from corner to corner, first top right, then bottom left, bottom right and finally top left. Diamond pattern is formed by changing colour of yarn.

Diagonal

Work diagonally from left to right forming squares, each consisting of 5 stitches. Work 1st and 5th stitch across 1 thread, 2nd and

4th across 2 threads, 3rd across 3 threads. In the next row the longest stitch is worked over the shortest and vice versa.

Fern

This stitch is worked in downward vertical rows. Start from the top left of the work. Insert the needle 2 holes down and 2 across and come out again one hole to the left. Insert the needle 2 holes up and 2 across and come out again one hole below the starting point of the previous stitch. Continue down the length of the row and work the next one immediately alongside. As this stitch is rapidly worked, it is useful for covering large areas of canvas.

Fishbone

This stitch is worked over 3 horizontal and 3 vertical threads of double thread canvas. Each long stitch is caught down with a short stitch across one double thread of canvas. It is worked in alternate rows from top to bottom and from the bottom upwards. The stitch makes a good grounding stitch and can be equally successful worked on single thread canvas.

C

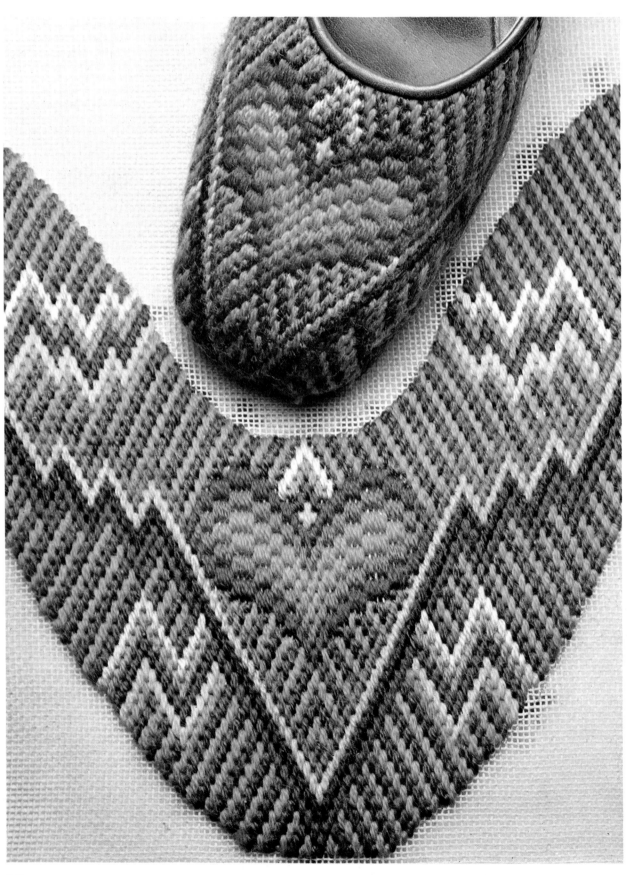

Florentine

This type of design is made of simple stitches in a zigzag or wavy line formation. The final result depends on the length of the basic stitch, the length of the stepping in the zigzag and the number of stitches in each step. Patterns are simple to work from a chart. Once the key line from the chart has been worked right across the canvas, the rest of the pattern is simply a matter of following this line and repeating it in different tones and colours. It is best done on single weave canvas. A frame is not necessary because the straight stitches used do not pull the canvas out of shape.

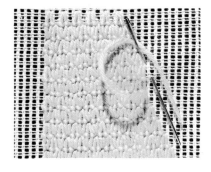

French

This very closely textured stitch is worked in diagonal rows from top left to bottom right. It makes a most attractive pattern for a background or to incorporate in a design. Work the main stitch from the bottom up over 4 threads then a central crossbar over it from right to left. Repeat the long

Carpet slippers in canvas work are both satisfying to make and quick to finish. Here a Florentine pattern has been combined with a central heart motif worked in blocks of satin stitch.

stitch in the same holes and then work the crossbar from left to right, starting from the same hole as the previous crossbar. Move down 4 holes to start next stitch.

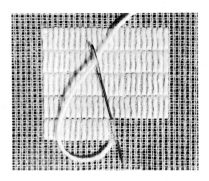

Gobelin (upright)

This is worked with straight up and down stitches, usually over 4 horizontal threads of canvas.

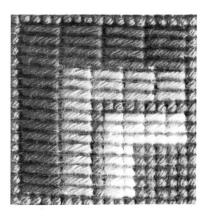

The L-shaped motif above would make an attractive belt or border. It is stitched in upright Gobelin worked over 4, 3 and 2 double threads of canvas. The background is worked over 1 thread. A three dimensional effect is obtained by using tones of one colour for the L-shape. It could be adapted as a geometric design.

Gobelin (plaited)

This stitch is worked in horizontal rows over 4 threads up and 2 across to the left. Work to the length of the area you want to cover leaving a space of 2 threads between each stitch. The

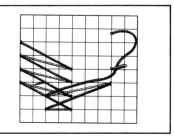

second row is worked 2 threads down and in the opposite direction, giving a plaited or woven effect (see diagram).

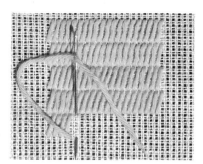

Gobelin (slanted)

This is similar to upright Gobelin, but worked over 2 vertical and 4 horizontal threads.

Hungarian

This stitch is worked in interlocking rows, over 2 and then over 4 horizontal threads.

C

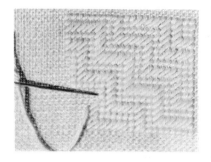

Jacquard

This stitch is generally used for covering a large area. Two colours may be used. It consists of one row of diagonal stitches worked over 2 horizontal and 2 vertical threads and a second row of half cross stitch. Change direction, upwards or horizontal, every six stitches.

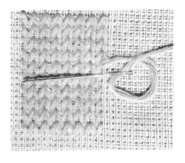

Knitting

This resembles chain stitch but it is worked in a similar way to stem stitch, in vertical rows. It is used only on double thread canvas. Bring the needle out at the top and insert it 2 holes down and across to the left. Bring the needle out 2 holes across and 1 hole up to the right and continue to the end of the row. The second row is worked in reverse from bottom to top. This

stitch can also be worked horizontally (2). Both versions can be used to cover large areas of canvas and can be easily worked by a beginner.

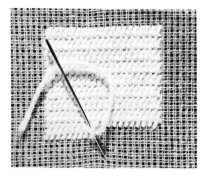

Knot

This slanting stitch is worked over 3 threads of canvas and caught down with a small slanting stitch across the centre of the stitch. The rows are interlocking.

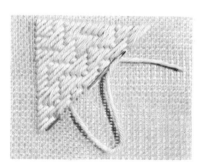

Milanese

This is formed from facing and interlocking triangles. It is worked diagonally in odd and even rows.
1st row Working downwards, make a backstitch alternately over 1 and over 4 diagonal threads.
2nd row Working upwards, backstitch over 3 and over 2 diagonal threads.
3rd row Working downwards, backstitch over 3 and over 2 diagonal threads.
4th row Working upwards, backstitch over one and over 4 diagonal threads.
In every row the longer stitches are worked under the shorter stitches of the previous row and

vice versa. This stitch is particularly suitable for covering large areas of canvas. It can be worked on canvas and then applied to velvet or the canvas and velvet can be worked as one piece of fabric. When completed the threads of canvas can either be pulled out or cut away.

Mosaic (1)

A stitch that can be worked in two ways to produce a similar effect. Work this version in diagonal lines. In the first row backstitch over one diagonal thread and continue in the same direction. In the second row, backstitch over 2 diagonal threads and continue in the same direction as shown in picture above.

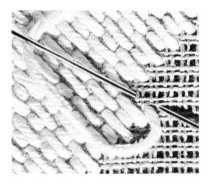

Mosaic (2)

This is worked in diagonal rows from top left to bottom right of the canvas in groups of 3 stitches; over 1, 2 and 1 threads of canvas. A chequered effect can be produced by using two different colours.

Cross stitch has been used for a modern director-style canvas chair cover.

Mosaic diamond
This is worked in rows from left to right over 1, 3, 5, 3 and 1 threads of canvas.

Parisian
This is a small, close filling stitch worked in interlocking rows over 1 and then over 4 horizontal threads.

Rice
This is a filling stitch which can be worked in one or two colours. It consists of ordinary cross stitch with the arms crossed by bars of cross stitch in the same or a different colour. Work the area in cross stitch, then work the first row of bars from left to right. Bring needle through 3rd hole down from top of work. Insert needle 2 holes up, 2 across to the right. Bring needle through 2 holes down, 2 across. Insert needle 2 holes up, 2 across to the right.

A tote bag worked in double cross stitch, rice stitch and satin stitch

Repeat to the end of row. Repeat the process from right to left to complete the row.

Rococo
This stitch gives an attractive starlike pattern and makes a good background stitch. The vertical rows are linked by horizontal stitches. Either 3 or 4 long stitches are all made from the same holes but held apart by the crossbars as shown. To start the second stitch bring the needle out 4 holes along from the starting point of the first stitch and fit the second row in between the sections of the first row.

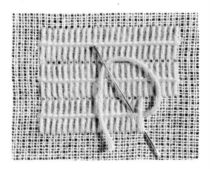

Rumanian or Roman
This stitch consists of two rows, linked with a row of stitches worked in a similar way to stem stitch. Work from left to right and work each stitch from the top down over 6 threads and then work the central crossbar over the stitch working from right to left, one hole out to either side of the long stitch. Complete the row in this manner. The second row is worked in the same way. To complete the stitch, a dividing row of stem stitch is worked from

right to left, moving one hole to the left and two back all the way. This dividing row can be worked in the same colour as the main stitch, or in a contrasting colour or yarn. On double weave canvas it creates a pretty effect to work the main stitch over narrow strips of ribbon.

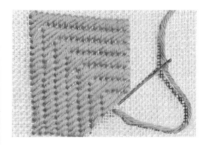

Satin stitch
This stitch is smooth and flat, it can be worked in several variations, in diagonal rows to give zigzag effects, into a square shape as cushion stitch or as four concentric triangles which makes a stylized flower head. The picture here shows the method used for turning a corner. Since satin stitch is quite long, crossing two, three or even more threads, it is not a good choice for cushions or chair covers because surfaces may catch and pull. Make sure that threads cover the canvas well, adding more strands of yarn if necessary. When using more than one strand, pull them all gently to ensure an even finish.

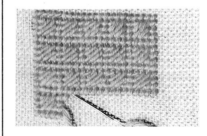

Scottish
Groups of diagonal satin stitch are set in an outline of half cross stitch. It can be worked in two tones of the same colour and used as a filling for fairly large spaces.

Cushion stitch, rice stitch and satin stitch design bordered with
long legged cross stitch and oblong cross stitch with bars.

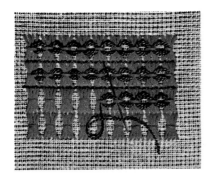

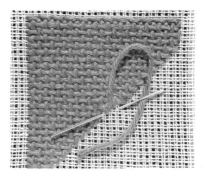

Shell

This is a compound stitch worked in three stages. First, sheaves worked over 6 vertical threads, 4 horizontal and then drawn together with one central horizontal stitch. Next, coils formed by taking one thread in a contrasting colour in a circle through the horizontal stitches as shown in picture. Finally, lines of backstitch are worked between the rows.

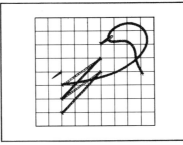

Spaces between the rows are filled with back stitches in a contrasting colour.

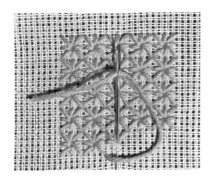

Star

This stitch is worked in diagonal rows with eight points in the completed star. Placing the needle through from the back of the work, begin with the top left point of the star. Take the needle through the centre hole from the front and then from the back, come through at the second point of the star, to the right. Work clockwise round the star until all points are completed.

Stem

Work from the bottom upwards over either 2 or 3 horizontal and vertical threads, then vice versa.

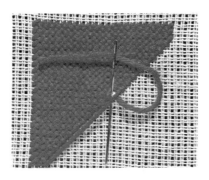

Tile

Work in diagonal rows over single or double thread canvas. First lay a foundation thread diagonally upwards over the required number of threads. Work downwards over this thread from right to left, taking each stitch over a single thread of canvas. Continue until required area is covered.
Both tile and web stitches are useful for grounding, both with a woven, fabric-like texture.

Web

Worked diagonally from right to left. Starting at top right hand corner, work first row downwards, returning upwards for the next row. Work each stitch of first row over 2 horizontal threads, starting the next stitch one thread to the left below first stitch. To turn work at end of row, take needle out 2 threads to the right and one below the horizontal stitch. On second row, take vertical stitches over 2 threads, taking each stitch one thread down, one to the right. A uniform texture is produced.

Catherine de Medici embroidery

This Italian embroidery stitch is also known as Madama. It is a type of counted thread work using thick natural coloured thread and open-weave fabric. It is similar to double running or Holbein stitch, being worked in two stages, the second part being worked over and under the preceding row.

C

Chain stitch

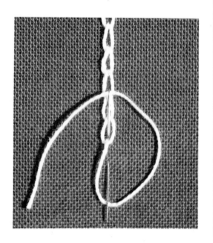

Work from right to left, making a chain of loops on the right side of the fabric and a line of back stitches at the back. Bring the needle through on the line of the design and hold the thread down either above or below the line with the left thumb. Insert the needle again at the point where it first emerged and bring the needle out a bit further along the line. Pull the needle through, keeping the thread under the point so that the next stitch holds it down in a loop. Continue working in same way for length of chain required.

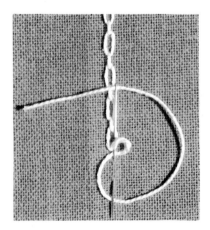

Cable chain

Start with a simple chain stitch. Then, holding the thread down with your left thumb, pass needle under thread and twist the needle into a vertical position so that the point comes over the top of the thread. Insert needle into fabric so that the working thread is twisted round it and make another chain stitch.

Daisy chain

This is worked in the same way as for detached chain stitch, but the detached chain is positioned to form a flower shape. It looks charming worked in groups of various colours on household linen or children's garments and can also be used for tiny leaves.

Detached chain

Make a chain stitch, then make a tiny stitch to hold the loop down. Leave a space and bring the needle out again to begin to make the next stitch.

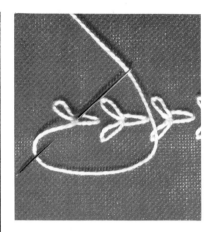

Russian

Make a chain stitch. Then, instead of continuing in a straight line, make the next stitch at an angle pointing upwards, then another, pointing downwards, catching each down with a tiny stitch. Bring the needle out again further along the line and repeat to make a line of stitches. This stitch can also be worked in groups as a filling stitch, or vertically in horizontal rows.

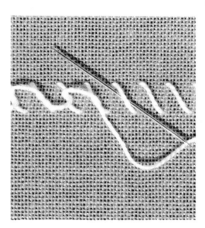

Serpentine

Work the first part of the stitch from right to left, making a line of slanting stitches evenly spaced. Working back from left to right, weave a second thread loosely over and under the parallel threads, taking the thread upwards and downwards.

Flower motifs worked in chain, detached chain, satin and stem stitches

C

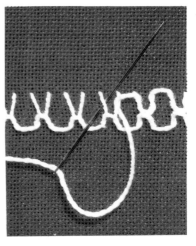

Sienese
First, from right to left, work a row of evenly spaced vertical stitches over an equal number of threads. Then, working from left to right, weave a second thread under, over and under the vertical stitches, pulling them together in pairs. When the lower row is completed work an upper row similarly to form the chain effect.

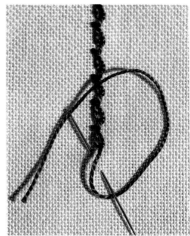

Twisted
For this stitch variation the needle is inserted at an angle to form the twist, giving a slightly raised line.

Chain stitch is ideal for embroidering curved or twisted lines. Here it gives the sparkling look of pine needles in winter with cones in satin stitch.

C

Colbert embroidery

This type of Italian design is worked on loosely woven fabric such as butter muslin. The motifs are embroidered in stem stitch, surface darning, double back or satin stitch while the background is filled with counted thread work. The example illustrated shows how bold and attractive effects can be achieved by keeping the motif simple and concentrating the stitching detail in the background in a similar way to Byzantine or Assisi embroidery.

Coral stitch embroidery

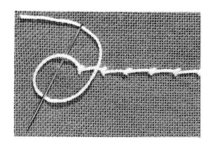

Working from right to left, bring thread up through the fabric and hold with the thumb of the left hand. Take a small stitch at right angles to the thread, going under and over it. Pull up to form a small knot. It can be used for outlining or working veins on leaves.

Cording

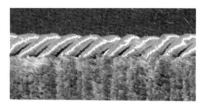

Silk cording in various widths is used on household furnishings. To finish an edge with cord, attach with slip stitch, stitching more closely at corners. You can also use cording to decorate cushions or covers by stitching it along lightly tacked guide lines that mark out the design. Take care to secure ends firmly.

Couching

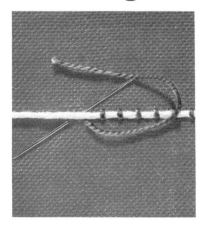

Couching is a form of simple surface decoration that has a multitude of uses. It is the method most frequently used in gold embroidery or for outlining appliquéd motifs in a contrasting shade.

This stitch will not withstand washing. First, secure the threads to be couched at the back of the work, draw them through to the right side and then catch into place, using a small stitch at regular intervals. Finally, take the ends through to the back of the work and secure in place. When couching two or more threads in place take care to prevent them twisting while you are working.

Cretan stitch

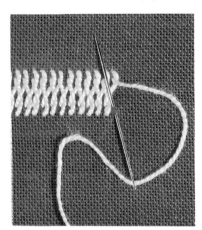

Work from left to right. Bring the needle through above the centre line of the design. Take a deep stitch immediately below this point and bring the needle up towards the centre line taking a small stitch and catching the thread under the needle. Make a second big stitch above the centre line and a little to the right of the bottom stitch and take a small stitch towards the centre of the design, catching the thread under the needle. Continue, taking great care that each stitch is as even as possible. Because of its close, woven effect, Cretan stitch makes a very effective filling stitch.

Cretan, open

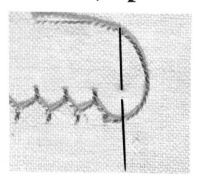

Work in exactly the same way as Cretan stitch, spacing the stitching at regular intervals. It is very important to keep the spacing even.

C

Crochet
Basic stitches

How to start

To start crochet, make a slip loop in the yarn and place it on the hook. Wrap yarn round first and second fingers of left hand. Insert hook under front loop and draw the back loop through to form a new loop, slipping it off fingers and transferring it to the hook. (1) Pull loop tight. The hook is held in your right hand as you would hold a pen or pencil (between thumb and first finger, letting hook rest against second finger, which controls it in moving through the stitches). Left hand is used to hold the work as it is made and to control the yarn from the ball. Control yarn by passing it over first and second fingers of left hand, then under third finger and round little finger, loosely letting the yarn flow.

Chain (ch)

Hold the stitch you have made between thumb and first finger of left hand. Pass hook from left to right under the yarn over your left hand fingers and round the hook (2). This is called 'yarn round hook' and is a most important part of all stitches. Draw yarn through loop on hook. This makes 1 chain (ch).

Double crochet (dc)

Make the required length of chain, plus two turning chain stitches (usually just called chain).

1st row Miss the first two chain. * Insert hook in next chain, yarn round hook, draw through loop (2 loops on hook), yarn round hook, and draw through both loops (1 loop on hook). This makes one double crochet. Repeat from * to end of chain. Turn.

2nd row 1 chain, miss first double crochet.* Insert hook through next double crochet (picking up both loops), yarn round hook, draw loop through (2 loops on hook), yarn round hook, draw loop through both loops on hook (1 loop on hook), repeat from * in every double crochet, working last double crochet into turning chain on previous row. Turn.

Repeat 2nd row until the work measures the required length. Fasten off. Do check the number of stitches at the end of each row, to make sure you have worked the full number of stitches.

Single crochet or slip stitch (ss)

This stitch is used chiefly for joins or in fancy patterns and it is the shortest in height of all the crochet stitches.

Make the required length of chain.

1st row Miss end ch, * pass hook through top loop of next ch, yrh, draw yarn through both stitches on hook, rep from * to end of ch. Turn. This makes 1ss.

2nd row 1ch, *1ss into next ss, rep from * working last ss into turning ch of previous row.

Repeat second row for length required. Fasten off.

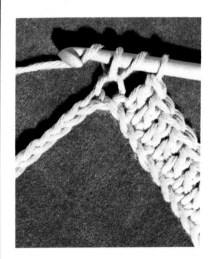

Treble (tr)

Make the required length of chain plus 3 turning chain.

1st row Miss first 3 chain * yarn round hook, insert hook into next

Afghan made up of squares of treble crochet in shades of yellow and green.

C

chain, yarn round hook, draw through one loop (3 loops on hook), yarn round hook, and draw through 2 loops (2 loops on hook), yarn round hook and draw through remaining 2 loops on hook (1 loop on hook). This forms 1 treble. Repeat from * to end of chain, turn.

2nd row 3 chain, miss the first treble * 1 treble in next treble, repeat from * to end of row, working last treble into third chain of turning chain, turn.

Repeat 2nd row until the work measures the required length. Remember to check the number of stitches you have worked at the end of each row to maintain the shape of your work. Always take care to draw up the first loop to its full height. Proper loop formation gives the finished stitch its full and soft appearance. If the top of the stitch is finished off too loosely a ragged effect will be produced.

Double treble (or long treble) (dtr)
To start off first work the required length of chain.

1st row Miss first 4ch, * yarn twice round hook—called y2rh—, insert hook into next ch, yrh, draw loop through ch, yrh, draw loop through first 2 loops on hook, yrh, draw loop through next two loops on hook, yrh, draw loop through last 2 loops on hook,

(this makes 1dtr), rep from * to end of ch. Turn.
2nd row. Work 4ch. Work 1 dtr into next dtr, rep from * to end of row, working last dtr into 4th ch or turning ch. Turn. Rep 2nd row for length required.

Double treble braid
Make 4ch, yrh twice and work a dtr into first of the 4ch, *yrh twice, insert hook into loop at base of last dtr and work a dtr, rep from * for length required.

Half treble (htr)
Make the required length of chain.

1st row Miss 2ch, * yrh, insert hook into next ch, yrh, draw through one stitch (3 loops on hook), yrh, draw through all loops on hook (1 loop on hook), (this makes 1htr), repeat from * to end of ch. Turn.
2nd row 2ch, * 1htr into next htr, repeat from * to last htr, 1 htr into 2nd of 2 turning ch. Turn. Rep. 2nd row for length required.

Buttonholes, crochet

Horizontal
Work until the position for the buttonhole is reached. When this is made as part of the main fabric of a garment, always finish at centre front edge, before working the buttonhole row. On next row, work a few stitches to where buttonhole is required, work two or more chain stitches to suit the size of the button, miss the corresponding number of stitches in row below, then pattern to end of row. On following row, work in pattern over chain stitches made in previous row to complete buttonhole.

Vertical
Work until position for buttonhole is reached. On next row work a

Striking chevron striped golfer and matching hat with a 'twenties look.

C

few stitches to where buttonhole is required, turn and work back and then work the required number of rows over these stitches to take size of button being used, ending at inner edge (see picture). Work in slip stitch down inner edge of rows to last complete row worked, work across remaining stitches for the same number of rows, then continue across all stitches.

Chevron stripes
Worked in four colours, A, B, C and D. Make an even number of chain.

Base row Into 2nd ch from hook work 1dc, 1dc into each of next 9ch, * work 3dc into next ch, 1dc into each of next 10ch insert hook into next ch and draw yarn through, miss 1ch, insert hook into next ch and draw yarn through, yrh and draw through all loops on hook, 1dc into each of next 10ch, rep from * to last 11 ch, work 3dc in to next ch, 1dc

into each of next 10ch, Turn.
1st patt row 1ch, dec one st by inserting hook into back loop only of next dc and drawing yarn through, insert hook into back loop only of next dc and draw yarn through, yrh and draw through all loops on hook, work 1dc in to each of next 9dc working into back loop only of each dc, *3dc into next dc, (which is the centre dc of the inc dc in previous row), working into back loop only, 1dc into each of next 10dc working into back loop only, dec in next 3dc by inserting hook into back loop only of next dc and drawing yarn through, miss 1dc, insert hook into back loop only of next dc and draw yarn through, yrh and draw through all loops on hook, 1dc into each of next 10dc working into back loop only, rep from * to end of row, dec one st in last 2dc by inserting hook into back loop only of last dc but one and drawing yarn through, insert hook into back loop only of next dc and draw yarn through, yrh and draw through all loops on hook. Turn. This row forms patt and is rep throughout. Keeping patt correct work 6 rows A, 6 rows B, 2 rows C, then 4 rows each in D, A, C, B, D, A and C. Fasten off leaving an end long enough to seam. Darn in all ends.

Decreasing

At the end of a row
To decrease one stitch at the side edge, miss the first stitch at the beginning of the row and insert the hook into the second stitch. Work to the last two stitches in the normal way, miss the next stitch and insert hook into last stitch. To decrease several stitches, work the row and turn, leaving the stitches to be decreased at the end

of a row, unworked.
There is a way to avoid ugly steps in your work where several stitches have to be decreased at once. For example, if three are to be decreased, work along the row to the last three stitches, miss the next two and work one slip stitch into the last stitch: turn with one chain, miss the slip stitch, work a double crochet into the next stitch, and then continue along the row in the normal way.

In the middle of a row
Work two double or treble crochet but keep the last loop of each stitch on the hook. Then draw a loop through all the loops that are remaining on the hook.

When making decreases in the middle of a row make sure you mark the spot with a length of contrasting coloured yarn. Then work the decrease in the two stitches before the marker if it is a right decrease, or in the two stitches after it, for a left decrease. For example, to decrease on double crochet, insert the hook into the first of these two stitches, yrh, and draw one loop through, keeping it on the hook. Insert the hook into the second stitch, yrh and draw another loop through so that there are three loops on the hook. Then, yrh, draw loop through all loops.

Fairytale crochet shawl, the centre worked in rows then edged with loops

48

C

Edgings

Angles
Make 4ch. Work 1dc and 1tr into the first of these 4ch, *turn work, 3ch, work 1dc and 1tr into previous tr, rep from * for length required.

Arches
Make 5ch and join into a ring with a ss. Into this loop work 6dc, 4ch, 1dc, turn. Rep from * for length required.

Clover
Work a number of chains divisible by 8, plus 1, for the required length.
1st row 1dc into 2nd ch from hook, * 1dc into next ch, rep from * to end. Turn.

2nd row 2ch, miss first dc, *3ch, miss 3dc and into next dc work 1dc, 5ch to form picot, (1dtr into same dc, 1 picot of 5ch) twice and 1dc all into same dc forming clover group, 3ch, miss 3dc, 1dc into next dc, rep from * to end. Finish off.
Thread ribbon between dc of first row.

Cluster
1st row Work along edge using double crochet. Break yarn.
The 2nd row is worked in the same direction as the 1st.
2nd row Join yarn with ss to first dc, 2ch, *1dc into next st, (yrh, insert hook into ch to right of dc just worked and draw through one loose st) 3 times into same stitch, yrh and draw through all loops, 1ch, miss 1dc, rep from * to end. Fasten off.

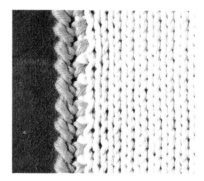

Crab
This is the simplest of all the variations of double crochet and can be worked backwards and forwards along an edge in rows, or continuously round a circular opening such as a cuff.
1st row Work along edge using double crochet. If working a circular edge, join with a slip stitch to the first stitch.
2nd row If the work is circular, work back along the round already made, making one double crochet in each double crochet and working from left to right instead of the normal right to left. If you are working in rows then do not turn the work but simply make one double crochet in each double crochet already made. Fasten off.

Crab, reversed
1st row Work along edge using double crochet. Turn.
2nd row 2ch, miss first dc, *1dc into next dc, rep from * to end. Do not turn.
3rd row Into each dc of previous row work 1dc, working from left to right. Fasten off.

Easy-to-crochet flower motifs, edgings and braid are useful for decorating table mats and napkins. Make the mats from crisp material such as linen which is colour-fast and easily laundered. Or simply stitch the crochet to ready-made mats. The choice of yarn depends entirely whether you want a delicate or chunky appearance.

C

Picot, lace

Work 2ch, * into the first of these 2ch insert hook, yrh, and draw through 1 loop. There are now 2 loops on hook. Into the loop nearest the hook point work 2ch. Slip both loops off hook and insert hook back only in to the loop further to the left. Without turning work, rep from * until edging is the required length. Finish off.

Do not turn work but rep from * until the edging is the required length. Finish off.

Small picot, worked direct on fabric

Begin by working 1dc into the fabric, * work 3ch, into the first of the 3ch work 2dc, miss a small section of edge of fabric and work 1dc into fabric. Continue in this way from * until all the edge has been worked. When working an edging all round a square or circular shape, finish at the point where you started and join to the first stitch with a slip stitch.

Picot, ring

*Work 5ch, into the first of these 5ch work 1tr. Without turning the work, rep from * until the edging is the required length. Finish off.

Picot, leaf

*Work 3ch, into the first of these 3ch work 3tr. Do not turn the work but rep from * until the edging is the required length. Finish off.

Picot, pointed

*Work 5ch, work 1ss into 2nd ch from hook, 1dc into next ch, 1htr into next ch, and 1tr into last ch.

Small picot

*Work 3ch, into the first of these 3ch work 2dc. Without turning the work rep from * until the strip is the required length. Finish off.

Steps

Make 3ch, work 3tr into the first of these 3ch, *3ch, turn, work 3tr into base of 3ch, rep from * for the length required.

Contrasting picot edging is used in a novel way to trim the yoke, cuffs and hem of this cosy knitted dressing gown. The crochet is worked on to the garment after the knitted sections are completed.

C

Twisted stitch

1st row Work along edge using double crochet. Turn.

2nd row *Insert hook into first dc, yrh and draw a loop through loosely, turn the hook on itself in order to twist the stitches, yrh and draw through all loops, rep from * to end. Fasten off.

Triple treble

Make 7ch. Work 1dc into 4th ch from hook, miss 2ch, 1tr tr into last ch. *3ch, 1dc into the first of these 3ch, 1tr tr into the second cross thread of previous tr tr, rep from * for length required.

Fabric stitches

Chevron pattern

Make a number of chain divisible by 6 plus 2 and 1 extra turning chain.

1st row (RS) Into 3rd ch from hook work 1dc, 1dc into each ch to end.

2nd row 1ch to count as first dc, miss first dc, 1dc into each dc to end working last dc into 2nd of first 2ch.

3rd and 4th rows As 2nd working last dc into first ch.

5th row 1ch to count as first dc, miss first dc, 1dc into each of next 2dc, 1RtF round 2nd dc of 2nd row, *miss 4dc on 2nd row, 1RtF round next dc on 2nd row, miss 2dc. on 4th row, 1dc into each of next 4dc on 4th row, 1RtF round dc on 2nd row next to last RtF, rep from * to last 5 sts on 4th row, miss 4dc on 2nd row, 1RtF round next dc on 2nd row, miss 2dc on 4th row, 1dc into next dc on 4th row, 1dc into first ch. 2nd to 5th rows form pattern.
(To work RtF or raised treble from the front, insert hook from front round stem of next tr, yrh and draw loop through, yrh and draw through 2 loops, yrh and draw through rem 2 loops).

Criss cross

Make a number of chain divisible by 4 plus 2 and 1 extra turning ch. Work 2 rows dc (you now have a number of stitches divisible by 4, plus 2).

3rd row 3ch, * miss next dc, 1tr into each of next 3dc, 1tr back into the missed dc, rep from * to last st, 1tr into last st.

4th row 1ch, 1dc into each st to end. The 3rd and 4th rows form the pattern.

Double double crochet

Make a chain of required length.

1st row Insert hook into 3rd ch from hook, draw yarn through, yrh, draw through 1 loop, yrh, draw through 2 loops on hook to form 1 double double crochet, work 1 double double crochet in each ch to end. Turn.

This row forms pattern and is repeated throughout, inserting the hook into each st of the previous row and beg each row with 2ch as turning ch.

Lattice stitch
Make a number of chain divisible by 4, plus 3.
1st row Into 2nd ch from hook work 1dc, work 1dc into each ch to end. Turn.
2nd row 2ch, 1dc into each dc to end. Turn.
3rd row As 2nd.
4th row 2ch, 1dc into each of next 2dc, insert hook from front to back of work in 1st st of 1st row, yrh, draw up long loop, yrh and pull through first loop on hook, miss 4 sts on 1st row, insert hook from front to back in next space, *yrh, draw up long loop, yrh and pull through first loop on hook, yrh and draw through all 3 loops on hook, miss 1dc behind this st, work 1dc in each of next 3dc, insert hook into same space as last loop worked, yrh, draw up loop, yrh and draw through first loop on hook, miss 4 sts on 1st row, insert hook from front to back in next space, rep from *, ending with 3dc. Turn. Rep 2nd row 3 times more.
8th row 2ch, 1dc into next dc, insert hook into st formed where loops join in 4th row, yrh, draw up loop, yrh and draw through first loop on hook, yrh and draw through both loops, miss dc behind this st, work 1dc into each of next 3dc, * insert hook from front to back in same place as first loop, yrh, draw up loop, yrh and draw through first loop on hook, insert hook in st joining next 2 loops on 4th row, yrh, draw up loop, yrh and draw through first loop on hook, yrh, draw through all 3 loops on hook, miss 1dc behind this st, work 1dc into each of next 3dc, rep from * to end, with last loop pulling yarn through first loop on hook, insert hook in last dc on 4th row, yrh, draw through loop,

Close-up photograph of lattice stitch showing how an attractive diamond pattern is formed on a close fabric background. It could be used to make a warm and pretty cover for a baby's cot or pram.

C

yrh, draw through all 3 loops on hook, miss 1dc behind this st, work 1dc into each of next 3dc. Turn. Rep 2nd row 3 times more.

12th row 2ch, 1dc into next 2dc, insert hook from front to back into st formed on 8th row, yrh, draw up loop, yrh, pull through first loop on hook, * insert hook into next joining loops in 8th row, yrh, draw up loop, yrh, draw through first loop on hook, yrh, draw through all 3 loops on hook, miss 1dc behind this st, work 1dc into each of next 3dc, insert hook in same place, yrh, draw up loop, yrh and draw through first loop, on hook, rep from * ending with 3dc. Turn.

Rows 5-12 form pattern and are repeated throughout.

Leaf
Make a number of chain divisible by 2, plus 1.

1st row Into 3rd ch from hook work 2dc, miss 1ch, *2dc into next ch, miss 1ch, rep from * to last st, 2dc in last st. Turn.

2nd row 2ch, * miss 1dc, work 2dc into 2nd dc of group, rep from * to end. Turn.

The 2nd row forms pattern and is repeated throughout.

Little leaf
Make a number of chain divisible by 2, plus 1.

1st row Into 3rd ch from hook

work 1dc, 1ch, 1dc into same st, miss 1ch, *1dc, 1ch, 1dc into next st, miss 1ch, rep from * to last st, 1dc, 1ch, 1dc into last st. Turn.

2nd row 2ch, * into ch between 2dc of previous row work 1dc, 1ch, 1dc, rep from * to end. Turn.

The 2nd row forms pattern and is repeated throughout.

Pineapple
Make a number of chain divisible by 4, plus 1 and 1 extra turning chain. Work 3 rows in dc (you now have a number of chain divisible by 4, plus 1).

4th row 1ch to count as first dc, 1dc into next dc, *(yrh, insert hook into next st, but 3 rows below (ie on 1st row) and draw a loop through, yrh and draw through 2 loops on hook) 6 times into the same st, yrh and draw

through all 7 loops on hook, 1dc into each of next 3dc, rep from * to end, but end with 2dc instead of 3. Work 3 rows in dc.

8th row 1ch to count as first dc, 1dc into each of next 3dc, * work a cluster as on 4th row, (working into the next st on 5th row) 1dc into each of next 3dc, rep from * to last st, 1dc into last st.

These 8 rows form the pattern.

Raised basket weave
Make a number of chain divisible by 4, plus 3.

1st row Into 2nd ch from hook work 1dc, 1dc into each ch to end. Turn.

2nd row 2ch, 1dc into each dc to end. Turn.

3rd row 2ch, work 1dc into each of next 2dc working into the back loop only of the row below, * work 1dc in to next dc inserting the hook in the corresponding st on the row below the previous row and drawing up a long loop, work 1dc into each of next 3dc working into back loop only of the row below, rep from * to end. Turn.

4th row As 2nd.

5th row 2ch, * work 1dc into next dc inserting the hook in the corresponding st on the row below the previous row and drawing up a long loop, work 1dc into each of next 3dc working into back loop only of the row below, rep from * to last 2 sts, work 1dc in next dc inserting hook and drawing up a loop as before, 1dc in back loop only of last dc. Turn.

Rows 2-5 form pattern and are repeated throughout.

Up and down
Make a number of chain divisible by 2, plus 1.

1st row Into 3rd ch from hook work 1dc, *1tr into next ch, 1dc into next ch, rep from * to end. Turn.

2nd row 2ch, *1dc into tr, 1tr into dc, rep from * to last st, 1dc in last st. Turn.

The 2nd row forms pattern and is repeated throughout.

Zigzag
Make a number of chain divisible

by 2, plus 1.

1st row 1tr into 4th ch from hook, 1ch, 1tr into the previous ch (ie 3rd from hook on foundation ch), *miss 1ch, 1tr into next ch, 1ch, 1tr into missed ch, rep from * to last ch, 1tr into last ch.

2nd row 3ch, 1tr into next 1ch sp, 1ch, 1tr into base of first 3ch, * 1tr into next 1ch sp (beyond the one which was worked into before), 1ch, 1tr back into previous 1ch sp, rep from * to end, 1tr into turning ch.

The 2nd row forms the pattern.

Filet crochet

Net ground
This consists of a fabric of spaces joined by trebles made by working, * 2ch, 1tr, rep from * for required length, ending with 1tr. The next and following rows are worked in the same way, working the trebles into the trebles of the previous row.

Beginning with block of trebles
To begin the first row with a block of trebles, make 3 extra chain to stand as the first treble and make next treble in the 4th chain from

hook. Complete first block of 4 trebles by working 1 treble in each of the next 2 chain.

Beginning with a space
To begin the first row with a space, make 5 extra chain of which the first 3 chain stand as the first treble. Then work 1 treble in the 8th chain from hook.

Decreasing space at beginning of row
Work last space of previous row, turn. On next row work 1 chain, 1 slip stitch in each of the next 2 chain stitches, 1 slip stitch in next treble, 5ch, miss 2ch, 1tr in next tr, *2ch, miss 2ch, 1tr in next tr, rep from * to end.

Decreasing space at end of row
At the end of the row where shaping is required do not work last space but turn work, make 5 chain and work 1 treble in 2nd treble of row below.

C

Increase space at beginning of row

Complete the row before shaping is required, turn work. On next row make 7ch (2 for base, 3 for side and 2 for top of space), work 1tr in last tr of previous row, * 2ch, miss 2ch, 1tr in next tr, rep from * to end.

Filet crochet worked with a chart

Working methods of filet crochet are very often given by means of a chart but, unlike knitting, each square on the chart does not necessarily represent just one stitch. A chart and row by row instructions are given for this sample. Each open square on the chart represents a 2 chain space plus a connecting treble and each cross represents a block of 2 trebles plus a connecting treble. Begin at the bottom right hand corner of the chart for the 1st row, turn work and read from left to right for the 2nd row, and so on.

Make 50 ch.

1st row Work 1ch into 8th ch from hook, (standing as first tr and first 2ch space), * 2ch, miss 2ch, 1tr in next ch, rep from * to end. Turn. (15 spaces).

2nd row (standing as first tr and first 2ch space), miss 2ch space, 1tr in next tr, 2tr in next 2ch space, 1tr in next tr, 2tr in next 2ch space, 1tr in next tr, (2 blocks),

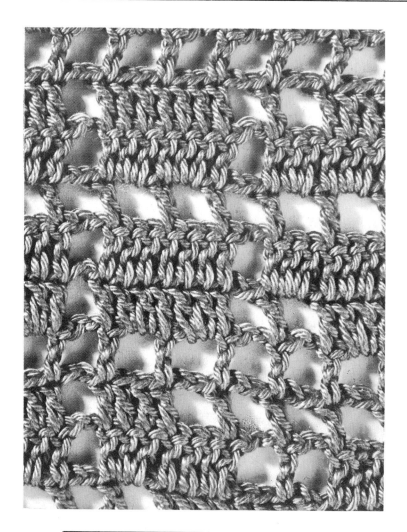

	✗	✗		✗	✗				✗	✗		✗	✗		14
	✗	✗			✗	✗		✗	✗			✗	✗		13
						✗		✗							12
	✗												✗		11
	✗	✗			✗	✗		✗	✗			✗	✗		10
		✗	✗		✗	✗		✗	✗		✗	✗			9
															8
		✗	✗		✗	✗		✗	✗		✗	✗			7
	✗	✗			✗	✗		✗	✗			✗	✗		6
	✗												✗		5
						✗		✗							4
	✗	✗			✗	✗		✗	✗			✗	✗		3
	✗	✗		✗	✗				✗	✗		✗	✗		2
															1

2ch, miss 2ch space, 1tr in next tr, (1 space), (2tr in 2ch space, 1tr in tr) twice, (2ch miss 2ch space, 1tr in tr) 3 times, (2tr in 2ch space, 1tr in tr) twice, 2ch, miss 2ch space (2tr in 2ch space, 1tr in tr) twice, 2ch, miss 2ch, 1tr in top of 3rd turning ch. Turn.

3rd row 5ch, miss 1tr and 2ch, 1tr in next tr, 2 blocks over next 2 blocks working 1tr in each tr, 1 space over 1 space, 2ch, miss 2tr, 1tr in tr (1 space over 1 block), 1tr into each of next 3tr, 2tr in 2ch space, 1tr in 1tr (1 block over 1 space) 1 space over 1 space, 2tr in 2ch space, 1tr in 1tr, 1tr in each of next 3tr, (1 block over 1 space, 1 block over 1 block), 1 space over 1 block, 1 space over 1 space, 2 blocks over 2 blocks, 2ch, miss 2ch, 1tr into 3rd of turning ch. Turn.

Continue working in this way from the chart, noting that 14 rows form one complete pattern repeat.

Increasing

Decorative increasing
Mark the place where the increase is to be made on the wrong side of the work. Then, working on the wrong side, make one chain before the marker if you want the increase to be on the

Demure summer blouse with loopy crochet panels and sleeves

C

left, or after the marker if you want it to be to the right. On the next row (right side) work the increase stitch into the chain made on the previous row.

Double increasing
Work as for increasing to right or left (see below), but work three stitches instead of two into the foundation stitch.

Increasing to left or right
Mark the place where the increase is to be made with a length of coloured thread. If the increase is to be made to the right, work two stitches into the stitch before the marker. If the increase is to be made to the left, work these stitches into the stitch after the marker. If the increases

are to be repeated in following rows, they are moved one stitch to the right, or one stitch to the left, depending on which side the increase is required.

Working two stitches into one
The simplest way to increase is to work two stitches into one. This can be done at each end of a row, or at one end only.
A second method is to add as many chain as the number of stitches to be increased, plus the turning chain at the end of the row. This way, an increase at the left side of the work is made at the end of a right side row and an increase at the right side of the work is made at the end of a wrong side row. When the work is turned, the new chain is worked the same as a commencing chain.

Jacquard

Crochet Jacquard patterns give working instructions in two ways, either by rows or by means of a chart. As working in several colours makes a close fabric it is advisable to use a crochet hook one size larger than one would normally choose for the thickness of the yarn. When a contrast colour has to be brought in, the last 2 loops of the last stitch in the main colour are drawn through with the yarn of the contrast colour, always keeping yarn on wrong side of work. When reverting to main colour, after working a group of stitches in a

contrast colour, the last 2 loops of the last stitch in the contrast colour are drawn through with the yarn of the main colour, always keeping the yarn on wrong side of work.

Loopy crochet

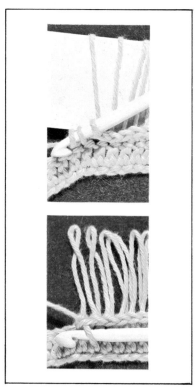

Fringing
Cut a piece of card which is strong enough not to bend to the required depth and sufficiently long to hold easily. It is not necessary to have the card the full

Long loopy fringing gives a luxurious finish to a light and delicate shawl.

C

length of a row. Several loops can be worked and then the card moved along.

To make a sample, cut a piece of card 2.5cm (1in) deep and 15cm (6in) long.

Work 20ch.

Work 2 rows dc. Turn.

3rd row Hold card in left hand, the base level with top of previous row. * Take yarn over top of card and down behind the card. Insert hook into the first st. and draw yarn from the back through 1 loop, yrh and draw through both loops, rep from * to end of row. Turn. Withdraw the card.

4th row 1ch, 1dc into each st. Work next row as 3rd row or if a less dense fringe is required, work several rows dc before again working a loop row. Long dainty fringes can be made by cutting a deep piece of card and by spacing the rows. Short thick fringes can be made by working over a narrow card with thick yarn and working every alternate row as fringe.

Working openwork rows
This effect is worked by pulling a long loop the required length out of a simple double crochet all along one row and then working the tips of the loops together on the following row with double crochet. Several rows may then be worked before another openwork row is made or, alternatively, a very lacy fabric can be achieved by working openwork rows on every alternate row.

To make a sample, work 20ch.

1st row Work 1dc into 2nd ch from hook, * 1dc into next ch, rep from * to end. Turn.

2nd row 1ch, * 1dc into next st. rep from * to end.

3rd row As 2nd.

4th row Insert hook into first st. yrh and draw through 1 loop on hook, yrh and draw through both loops and drawing the new loop out to the required length, * insert hook into next st, yrh, draw through 1 loop, yrh, draw through long loop pulling it up to the required length, slip hook out of loop and rep from * to end of row. It may be found that it is easier to keep the loop on the hook until several are made so that it is simple to keep them the same length.

5th row Work a number of chain the same length as the loop, insert hook into top of loop, yrh, draw through 1 loop, yrh, and draw through both loops, * insert hook into next loop, yrh and draw through 1 loop, yrh and draw through both loops, rep from * along row to end.

Work several rows dc before repeating 4th row as required.

Mitred corners

Pointed
To make a separate band having a pointed mitred corner, first measure the length of band required and make the necessary number of chain. Mark stitch which is to be the innermost point of corner with coloured thread. The band is worked from the inside to the outside edge.

1st row (Right side.) Work 1dc in to 2nd ch from hook, then work 1dc into each ch to the last ch before the marked corner ch, work 2ch and continue working 1dc into each ch to end. Turn.

2nd row 2ch, work 1dc into each dc and 1dc into each of the 2ch at corner. Turn.

Continue in this way, working 2ch at corner on every RS row working 1 more dc on each RS row before making the 2ch and working 1dc into each of these 2ch on WS rows until the band is the required depth. Fasten off. Any number of chain may precede and follow the corner stitches, depending on the angle of the corner, but always work one more stitch before corner chain on each RS row.

Rounded
Prepare the band as for pointed mitred corner.

1st row (Right side.) Work 1dc in to 2nd ch from hook, then 1dc into each ch to marked corner st, work 3dc into corner st and 1dc into each ch to end. Turn.

2nd row 2ch, work 1dc into each dc to end. Turn. Repeat these two rows until band is the required depth, working 3dc into centre stitch of the three corner stitches on each RS row.

Open work stitches

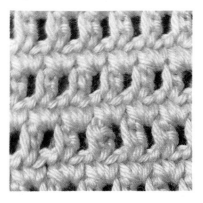

Chainmail
Make a number of chain divisible by 2, plus 1.

1st row Into 2nd ch from hook

work 1dc, 1dc into each ch to end. Turn.

2nd row 3ch, miss 1st dc, * insert hook in next st, yrh, draw yarn through, yrh, draw through first loop on hook, yrh, draw through first loop on hook, yrh, draw through 2 loops on hook, 1ch, miss 1dc, rep from * ending 1tr in last st. Turn.

3rd row 2ch, work 2dc into each space of previous row to end. Turn. Rows 2 and 3 form pattern and are repeated throughout.

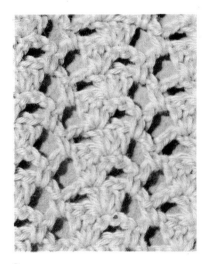

Crazy

Make a number of chain divisible by 6, plus 2.

1st row Into 2nd ch from hook work 1dc, * 2ch, miss 2ch, work 3tr into next ch, 2ch, miss 2ch, 1dc into next ch, rep from * ending with 1tr in last ch. Turn.

2nd row *2ch, 1dc into space before 3tr group of previous row, 2ch, 3tr into 3rd tr of previous row, rep from * ending with 1tr in space between last dc and turning ch. Turn.

The 2nd row forms pattern and is repeated throughout.

Fan stitch

Make a number of chain divisible by 8, plus 1.

1st row Into 2nd ch from hook work 1dc, work 1dc into each ch to end. Turn.

Fan stitch, shown here in close-up, would make up beautifully into a huge fringed stole. Begin and end with two rows of trebles and allow five extra trebles at each end of the rows to give a border effect, then complete it with a luxurious length of fringe.

C

2nd row 2ch, 1dc into each dc to end. Turn.

3rd row 5ch, miss 3dc, * (1tr, 3ch, 1tr) into next dc, 2ch, miss 3dc, 1tr in next dc, 2ch, miss 3dc, rep from * ending with 1tr in last st. Turn.

4th row 2ch, * 2dc in next space, 1ch, 5dc in next space between tr, 1ch, 2dc in next space, 1ch, rep from * ending with 2dc in last space, omit last ch and work 1dc in turning ch. Turn.

5th row 2ch, 1dc in first dc, 1ch, work petals thus: * yrh, insert hook into 1st dc of 5dc of previous row, yrh, pull through loop, yrh, put hook into same dc, yrh, pull through loop, yrh, put hook into same dc, yrh, pull through loop, yrh, pull through all 7 loops on hook, rep from * into each of next 4dc, 1ch, miss 1ch and 2dc, work 1dc into next 1ch space, 1ch, miss 2dc and 1ch, rep from * ending with 1dc and omitting last ch. Turn.

6th row 5ch, *1dc in space between 2nd and 3rd petals of next petal group, 2ch, 1dc in space between 3rd and 4th petals, 2ch, (1tr, 2ch, 1tr) all into next dc between petal groups, 2ch, rep from * omitting 2ch and 1tr from last rep. Turn.

7th row 2ch, 3dc into first space, work 2dc into every space to end, 1dc in 2nd ch of turning ch. Turn. Rows 2-7 form pattern and are repeated throughout.

Triangle
Make a number of chain divisible by 3, plus 2.

1st row Into 2nd ch from hook work 1dc, 1dc into each ch to end. Turn.

2nd row 4ch, * miss 2dc, work 1tr into next dc, insert hook into 2nd missed dc behind tr just worked, work 1tr, 1ch, rep from * ending 1tr. Turn.

3rd row 2ch, miss first tr, work 1dc into each st to end, ending 1dc into 3rd ch of turning ch. Turn. Rows 2 and 3 form pattern and are repeated throughout.

Spiral crochet

Work 20ch.
1st row Work 2tr into 4th ch, * 3tr in next ch, rep * to end of ch. Cut yarn and finish off the spiral. Use as a trimming for a scarf or cap, zip tab or key ring.

Tubular crochet

Foundation chain
Commence with the number of chains which are required to give the total circumference of

the article being made. Join into a ring with a slip stitch into the first foundation chain. Continue working in rounds with the chosen stitch for the necessary depth. It is advisable to mark the beginning of the first round with a coloured thread, so that you know where to finish. The right side of the work is always facing you.

Rib
Work each round in double crochet on a foundation chain joined into a ring but insert the hook into the back loop only of each double crochet.

Rose stitch
Work each round in half trebles on a foundation chain joined into a ring.

Russian
Work each round in double crochet on a foundation chain joined into a ring.

Twisted
Work a foundation chain joined into a ring. Insert hook in centre of foundation chain with the hook pointing downwards (instead of the normal way with the hook facing you), pass the hook over the yarn on the left index finger and pull yarn through chain, pass the yarn over the hook from left to right (instead of the normal way from right to left), pull yarn through 3 loops on hook. This completes one stitch. On following rounds insert hook through both loops of stitch in previous round.

V-neckline in crochet

The deeper the 'V', the more gradual the shaping. A high 'V' must decrease more rapidly in order to complete the shaping

before reaching shoulder level. Mark position of centre stitch and work each side separately.
1st row (Right side.) 2ch, work 1dc into each dc, miss 1dc before marked centre st, work 1dc in centre st. Turn.
2nd row 2ch, work in dc to end. Repeat 2nd row twice more.
5th row 2ch, work 1dc into each dc, miss last dc but one at neck edge, work 1dc in last dc. Turn. Repeat rows 2-5 until required number of stitches have been decreased at neck edge, then continue without shaping, if necessary, to a depth of 25.5cm (10in), the average depth for a 'V' neck. With RS of work facing, rejoin yarn to centre st.
1st row 2ch, miss 1dc, work 1dc in to each dc to end. Turn.
Work 3 rows without shaping. Repeat these 4 rows to match first side.

Cross stitch

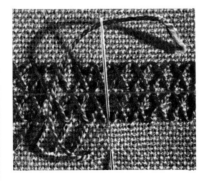

This should be worked on an even-weave fabric because this makes it easier to count threads and the whole effect of the stitch

depends on its regularity. Ideally each stitch should make a perfect square, being worked down and across over an equal number of threads. The most even finish for filling large areas is obtained by working a row of diagonal stitches in one direction and then completing them by working another row in the opposite direction.

Filling small areas
If there is only a small area to cover, you can use the alternative method where one stitch is completed at a time, but this will look less even.

Cross stitch variations

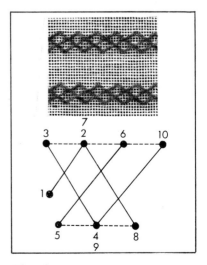

Algerian
Worked from left to right on an uneven number of threads. Work stitches upwards and downwards, following diagram.

65

C

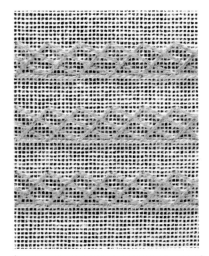

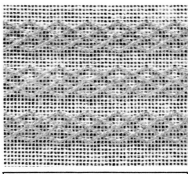

Bring needle out at point no.1 on diagram and proceed, following diagram to no.15. The next row fills the horizontal spaces left in the first row.

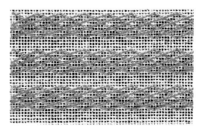

upwards, point no.5 is 8 threads below to the left. For no. 6 take an oblique stitch 4 threads above no.1, return to no.7 on wrong side and take a vertical stitch to no.8. Continue to no.10, following diagram. Continue working steps 3 to 9.

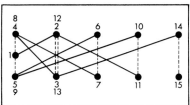

Belgian

Worked from left to right. Follow the diagram from no.1 to no.8, then repeat, beginning at no.2. Dotted lines indicate wrong side of work.

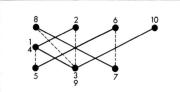

Double

Work from left to right. Follow diagram from no.1 to no.10, then continue working from no.6 to no.10. Dotted lines indicate wrong side of work.

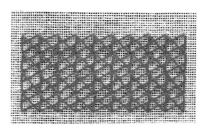

Russian

Work from left to right. Following diagram, steps 1 to 15. Then repeat steps 11 to 15. At the end of one row, work as for beginning but in opposite direction so that both ends of row correspond.

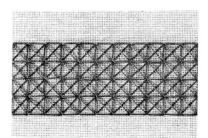

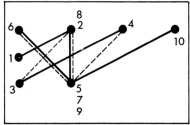

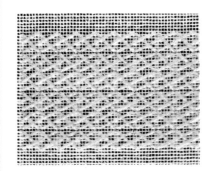

Boxed

Worked from left to right and vice versa in an upwards direction.

Montenegran

Worked from left to right. From no.1 count 8 threads to the right and 4 upwards, making step no.3 come out 4 threads below the starting point. Point no.4 is 16 threads to the right and 8 threads

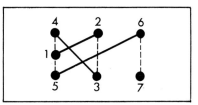

Slav

Work from left to right. Take yarn 6 threads to right and 3 up, no.2

A gay, colourful design in simple cross stitch. This photograph is very much enlarged, the actual size of the section shown would measure about 10cm (4in) square when worked on double thread canvas. It can be embroidered in either tapestry, crewel or knitting wool.

C

then take yarn 6 threads down, no.3. The yarn is then taken diagonally back and 3 threads up from first point, no.4, then 6 threads down, no.5. Next stitch on right side is made 12 threads diagonally to the right and 6 up, no.6, then taken 6 threads down to point no.7. Continue working steps 3 to 7. Stitches on wrong side are marked with dotted lines.

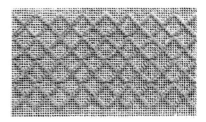

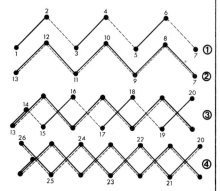

Two sided

Worked in two journeys one way, then two journeys back, from left to right. In first row take yarn 4 threads across and 4 threads up, see step 1 on diagram. When working return row, no.2, take needle under stitches made in first row, marked with dotted lines. Start third row with a half stitch, see step no.3. The fourth return row completes the stitch, see step no.4.

Cut work (Richelieu)

The motifs are surrounded with closely worked buttonhole stitch linked with bars, the rest of the fabric being cut away. Use *coton*

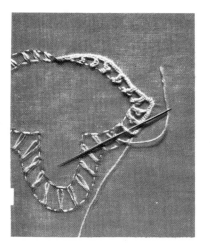

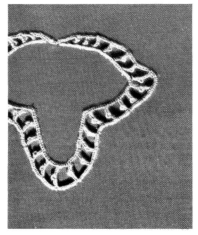

à broder or two or three strands of stranded cotton depending on thickness of fabric being stitched: this should be either linen or good quality, firmly woven cotton. Apply the design using a commercial transfer or dressmaker's carbon paper. Tack the fabric on to stiff, strong paper so that it is well stretched with the grain of the fabric straight and work small running stitches round lines of design on fabric only, until you come to a bar. Fasten thread with a tiny back stitch on right side of fabric without cutting off thread, pass over the bar and pick up two or three threads of fabric, pass back to far side and continue running stitches. Bars are worked at close intervals, following curves of design. Cover running stitches and foundations for bars with closely worked buttonhole stitch. To give more strength and a

raised edge this is worked over a laid thread of one strand of *coton à broder* or two or three strands of stranded cotton. When a bar is reached, pass another thread across the two existing ones and cover all three threads with buttonhole stitch, not picking up fabric underneath. Bars can be decorated with picots (1). Fasten off by taking a few running stitches along line of design where they will be covered with buttonhole stitch. When embroidery is complete unpick tacking stitches and remove paper from back of work. Press embroidery carefully on wrong side over a soft pad, using damp cloth. Trim fabric away as close as possible to buttonhole stitched edges, taking care not to damage stitching. Use very sharp, pointed embroidery scissors.

Czechoslovak embroidery

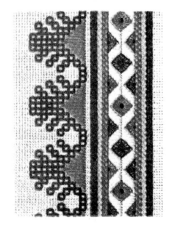

This is worked on even-weave fabric in both geometric and floral styles in a variety of stitches including cross, satin and stem stitches, surface darning and counted thread work.

Modern interpretation of cut work embroidered in crisp white on blue linen.

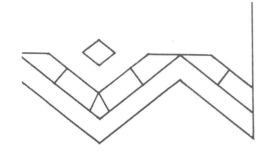

D

Striking darning design worked in zigzags between lines of drawn threads. First withdraw two threads, leave nine, withdraw two more, leave sixteen and so on. Use matt embroidery thread or pearl cotton.

D

Deruta embroidery

Italian counted thread embroidery which is worked on delicate open-weave fabric. Designs are mostly geometric, predominantly squares.

Dot stitch

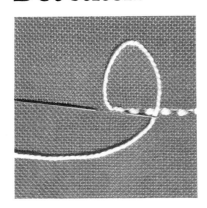

This is worked from right to left. Two back stitches are worked into the same hole. It can either be used as a line or filling stitch.

Drawn thread work

This is based on the removal of either the warp (lengthwise) or the weft (crosswise) threads from a precise, even-weave fabric. The remaining threads are grouped together into patterns by knotting or interlacing. Pearl cotton, *coton à broder*, soft embroidery cotton or stranded cotton can be used, they should be chosen in relation to the thickness of the fabric.

Stitches

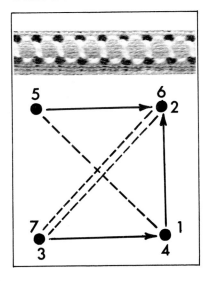

Four sided
Withdraw 1 horizontal thread, leave 5, then withdraw a second horizontal thread. Work from right to left, making stitches in order shown in diagram.

Four sided (reversed)
Withdraw threads as for four sided stitch, then work from left to right, following diagram in reverse so that the dotted lines are the ones that lie on top of the work.

Four sided (criss cross)
Withdraw threads as for four sided stitch, then working from left to right, make one half cross as shown in picture, then make two vertical stitches between the two drawn threads.

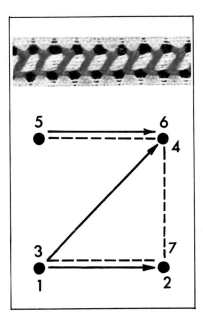

Four sided (diagonal)
Withdraw threads as for four sided stitch, then work from left to right, following the diagram.

D

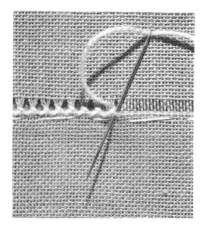

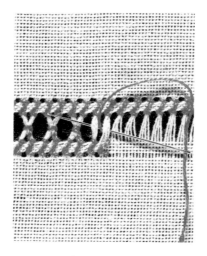

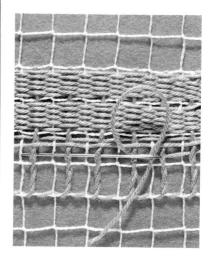

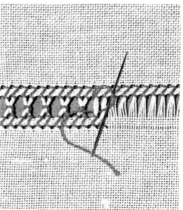

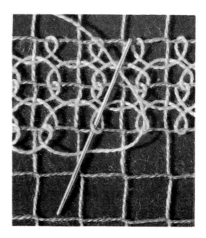

Handkerchief hem stitch

This is the best-known of the traditional drawn thread stitches. Following grain of fabric, mark rectangle the size required for finished area with line of tacking stitches. Measure inwards from this line to depth of hem required. With a needle, lift one horizontal thread and snip it carefully with scissors. Still using needle, unpick this thread, working away from centre towards corners. Do not unpick any further than corners, but leave ends long enough to darn back into fabric to avoid fraying. Similarly draw a thread on all four sides until drawn threads meet and form a square hole at corners. These spaces can be buttonhole stitched, overcast or decoratively filled. Withdraw one to three threads. Measure hem depth outwards from line of tacking stitches and mark with a second line of tacking. Trim off excess fabric outside this second line, leaving just a little to fold inside hem, about 1.2cm ($\frac{1}{2}$in) for a traycloth. Fold crease on first line of tacking and then on second to form hem. Tack hem to within one thread of exposed threads. Mitre corners. Working on wrong side, from left to right, with end of thread inside hem, insert needle from right, picking up four of the exposed threads. Pull needle through and pick up two threads of the turned hem. Make sure that the same two horizontal threads are picked up all along the hem.

Knotting threads

Draw out 1 thread, leave 4, draw out 8, leave 4, draw out 1. Work on wrong side, from left to right. First row is worked in diagonal four sided stitch. Next, knot the broad band of drawn threads in groups of 4 as shown in pictures 1 and 2, at the same time working the bottom row in diagonal four sided stitch.

Fillings

Check

Draw out 8 threads and leave 6,

horizontally and vertically. Neaten sides with overcasting. Finish alternate small central squares with satin stitch. Finally interlace the groups of 6 threads as shown.

Darning

This is a drawn thread filling, shown here on net for maximum clarity. Work backwards and forwards, over and under alternate threads.

Loop stitch

As a drawn thread filling this is worked in the same way as on net, as shown here. For filling the square empty space formed where drawn threads meet, first darn in ends, then buttonhole stitch or overcast edges of square. To work filling, first fix thread to left side of reinforced hole, then by looping

Handkerchief hem stitch makes a neat finish to this table mat and napkin set. The petals of the marguerites are embroidered in padded satin stitch using three strands of cotton in the needle and the centres are filled with a mass of French knots. The leaves and stems are worked in satin stitch using shaded cotton for additional interest.

D

thread to upper edge, right edge and lower edge, finishing back on left.

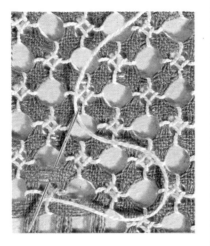

Loop stitch, worked diagonally

Draw out 6 threads, leave 6 and draw out 6 again, both horizontally and vertically. This produces a regular grid which is then decorated with diagonally worked loop stitch. In moving from one space to the next the thread is hidden by the fabric.

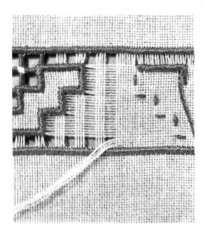

Russian overcast

A simple design is drawn on squared paper, then outlined on fabric with small running stitches. Overcast the outer edges, then round the contours of the design. Draw out background threads in groups of 4, cutting threads to be drawn close to outline very carefully. Overcast remaining threads.

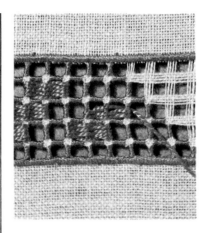

Russian overcast, (darning filling)

Draw out design on squared paper, then prepare section to be worked, drawing out and leaving threads in alternate groups of 4. Overcast upper and lower edges and background threads, then work darning filling. This can be easily adapted into simple geometric patterns.

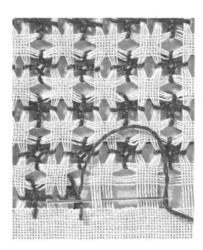

Star

Draw out 8 threads and leave 8, horizontally and vertically. Work loop stitch in horizontal lines to fill spaces, taking up the outside threads in groups of 4. In this way the groups of 8 threads are divided in half, producing a decorative star motif.

Sunray

Draw out 9 threads and leave 9, horizontally and vertically. Next,

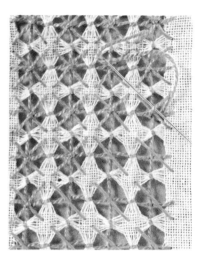

using a contrasting colour, knot horizontal and vertical threads. Then work diagonally from left to right, passing over 1st, 2nd and 3rd, under 4th, 5th and 6th, over 7th, 8th and 9th threads of fabric. Finally, work diagonally from right to left in the same way, knotting intersections.

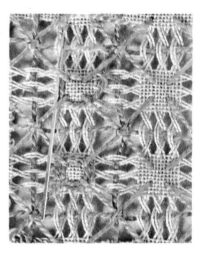

Wheel

Draw out 12 threads and leave 12, horizontally and vertically. The horizontal and vertical threads are then interlaced in pairs. Then the diagonal threads are worked, knotted at the intersections and passed under the centres of the solid squares of fabric as shown. Finally, these squares are decorated with wheels, formed by taking thread three times round under the diagonal threads.

Embroidery on net

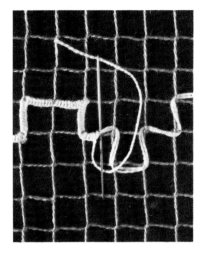

Buttonhole edging

Buttonhole stitch can be worked on netting to form a striking geometric pattern which can be used very effectively for edging. First, wind one or two threads of yarn along the line of the design and then fasten them firmly to the net with buttonhole stitch.

Fillings

Daisy

Start at the knot which is to be the centre of the flower, then work two diagonal loops as illustrated to form the petals, finally work round the central intersection to pull the petals together.

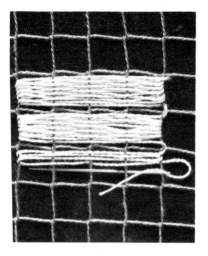

Darning stitch

Fasten working thread to a knot in the net and then weave over and under the bars of the net as illustrated. Continue backwards and forwards until required shape is filled. Finish off neatly at the back by weaving in the end. This is important because the work will be visible from both the front and the back.

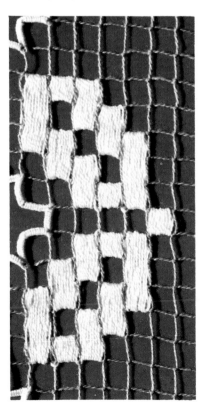

Leaves worked in darning stitch over varying numbers of squares.

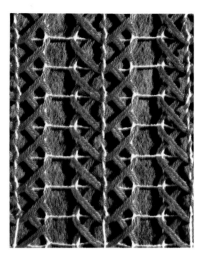

Geometric

This design is made by working a series of diamonds, each one on a base of four knots of net.

Secure the thread to the knot which forms the apex of the diamond, then work over and under the vertical and horizontal bars of net as shown. When diamond is finished, wind the thread round the centre bar down to the knot below, to begin the next diamond. This motif is shown worked vertically but can be worked from left to right.

Linen stitch

This can be used either as a filling stitch or on its own to form shapes. It consists of rows of alternated running stitch, worked first vertically and then horizontally and interwoven. Each square always contains an equal number of threads.

Fasten thread to a knot in the net and working vertically, pass the thread alternately over and under the bars of the net. This can be worked in one square only or over several squares to fill a large area. When laying the vertical threads remember that the strands to left and right of a vertical bar of net must both run in and out in the same way, as the bar of net will form the alternating thread. In this way the pattern of the horizontal threads is not broken. Lay the horizontal threads by

E

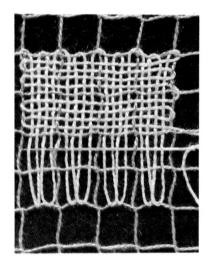

picking up alternate vertical threads. Work as many horizontal threads to each square as vertical ones to form an even filling.

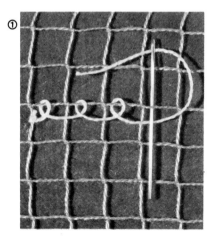

Loopy filling

(1) Fasten the thread with a knot and work a series of loops across the net over the top bar of each square, carrying the thread over all the vertical bars in between the loops.

(2) When you reach the end of a row, loop the thread round the vertical bar of that square and work back again, making a series

Darning stitch, worked in a traditional pattern on net is used for a decorative insertion on a linen tablecloth.

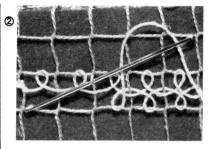

of loops over the bottom bar of each square. This time take the thread under the vertical bars between loops.

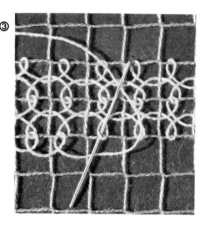

(3) Continue working the pattern taking the new loops through those already worked.

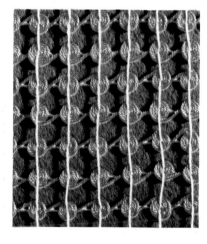

Spiral

This is worked in rows, left to right. Turn work after each row so that you are always working in the same direction. Secure thread with a knot at left edge of work. Point needle downwards diagonally behind the first knot and

bring the thread out to the lower right of knot. Then insert needle from right to left under the vertical bar above the knot, then from left to right, under the same bar below knot. Wind thread two or three times round centre knot, working under the vertical bars and over the horizontal bars of the net.

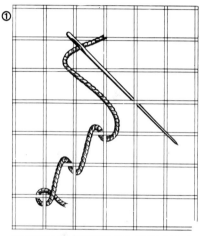

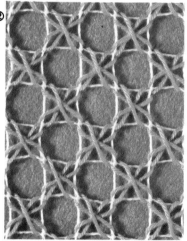

Star

Knot thread at bottom left hand corner of net.

1st row Work diagonal stitches from bottom left to top right of each square (1).

Next row Work back the way you came intertwining thread with that of first row. Working parallel to this, cover the area to be embroidered. Turn work and complete another series so that they intersect the first (2).

E

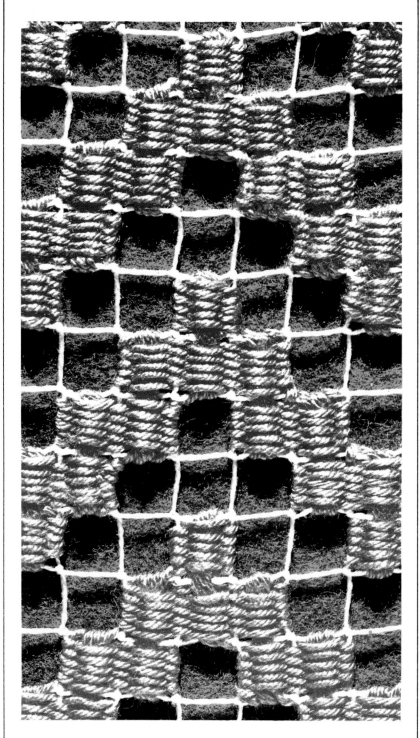

Embroidery on net is a very old craft which was originally worked in white or a natural colour on a matching background, but in modern adaptations of the technique contrasting shades are introduced. In this example a zigzag effect is produced by darning over two squares at a time and stepping up or down by one square of net.

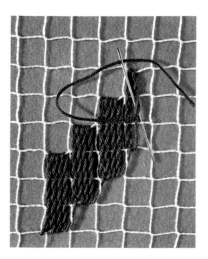

Twisted

This is a variation of darning stitch. Knot thread to net to fasten and take it up as a vertical foundation over the number of squares you wish to cover. Loop thread under horizontal bar of last square. Form twist by taking thread from right to left, and needle from left to right under this vertical thread and the horizontal thread of the net. Continue until required area is covered.

Motifs

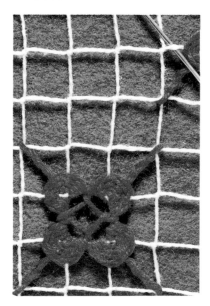

Flower

To work petals, stretch thread diagonally from one corner of a square to the other and overcast it. Then weave under and over bars of net and overcast thread. Finish off at back with a knot. Repeat the process in the other three corners of the square, then decorate the flower centre with looped stitches.

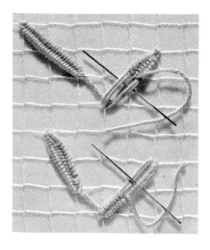

Leaf (darning stitch)

For the lower leaf shown make foundation by taking a double loop of thread under one knot of the net, passing over mesh diagonally. To fill in the leaf, darn under and over these threads as shown. For upper leaf on right work similarly but this time darn over a central foundation thread. Do not pick up net underneath in either case.

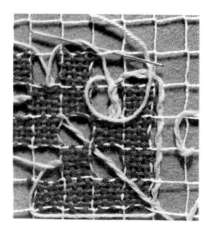

Leaf (outlined linen stitch)

First work leaf in linen stitch. Next define, veins and outline of

leaf with a single thread, taken over and under net as shown. Overcast to strengthen outline. To keep tension of stitches even tack work on to card to support it while you work.

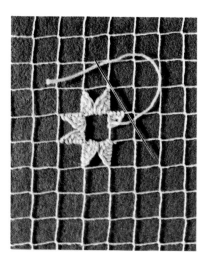

Star flower

Each motif is worked in buttonhole stitch round a central square of net. To work first point, start from corner of central square, make first stitch along next horizontal thread, then take thread across to side of square at right angles to it as illustrated. Work from side to side until first point is filled, then continue to make remaining points.

Triangle (buttonhole stitch)

Mark outline of triangle with thread. Work alternately to right and to left in buttonhole stitch keeping tension tighter at apex of triangle and looser at base.

Triangle (darning stitch)

Mark outline of triangle with thread. To fill triangle work from top in darning stitch taking needle alternately to the right and to the left. This forms a central indentation as shown.

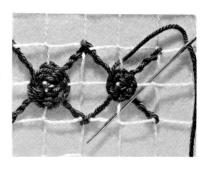

Wheel (darning stitch)

Prepare the foundation by running the thread out in four spokes, then overcast back to centre. Working from centre, weave thread in and out of the threads of foundation and net. Continue, alternating stitches over and under until wheel is filled. Finish with small knot at back.

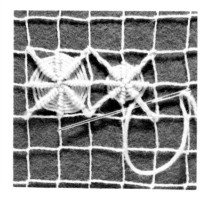

Wheel (ribbed)

Prepare foundation as for darning stitch wheel. Then work back stitches round and round from centre over threads of net and foundation to form a solid wheel.

E

E

Wheel (running stitch)
Prepare foundation as for darning stitch wheel. Working from centre, make rounds of running stitch, taking thread over foundation threads and under threads of net.

Embroidery on tulle

Tulle is sold in varying widths and is made of either nylon or silk. Both are suitable for embroidery and make an ideal background for embroidery for wedding veils, christening robes and lingerie. Simple geometric shapes and patterns are usually worked on the coarser meshes without a pattern. Soft thread should be used, mercerized sewing cotton such as Sylko Perlé no.3 or no.5 is suitable for coarse meshed tulle and nos. 8 or 12 for finer meshes. The chosen design is copied on to tracing paper, the tulle placed upon it and a piece of firm card placed under the paper. Tack the three layers together, so that the design can be seen and the card supports the tulle (care should be taken not to pucker the fabric). For large areas of embroidery, such as a wedding veil, architect's linen should be used. The design is copied on to the linen and the tulle tacked to it. A blunt needle such as a crewel needle

should be used in proportion to the mesh. To begin working, run needle through mesh, leaving a loose end about 8cm (3in) long. After embroidery has been completed darn end invisibly into back of work.

Simple stitches

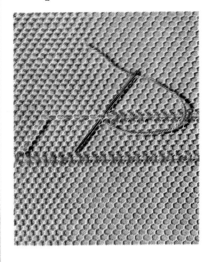

Cording
First work a running stitch guide line, then oversew this as illustrated. This stitch provides a bolder line than the normal running stitch outline.

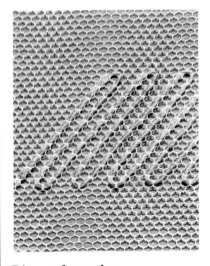

Diagonal running
Pick up every other mesh of the tulle, diagonally. To work this as a filling stitch make several parallel rows up and down,

missing one row of holes between each stitched row and using a thicker yarn.

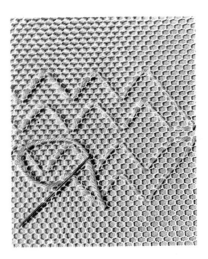

Running
Pass needle over one mesh of tulle and under the next, alternately. Running stitch is mostly used for defining outlines but can also be worked as a filling.

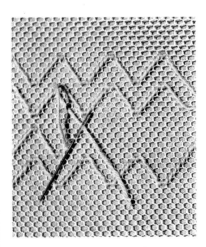

Stem
This is worked in the same way as it would be embroidered on fabric. For each stitch pick up one mesh of tulle, keeping thread to right or left of needle depending on direction of slope being worked.

Loopy filling with buttonhole stitch border worked in soft embroidery cotton

E

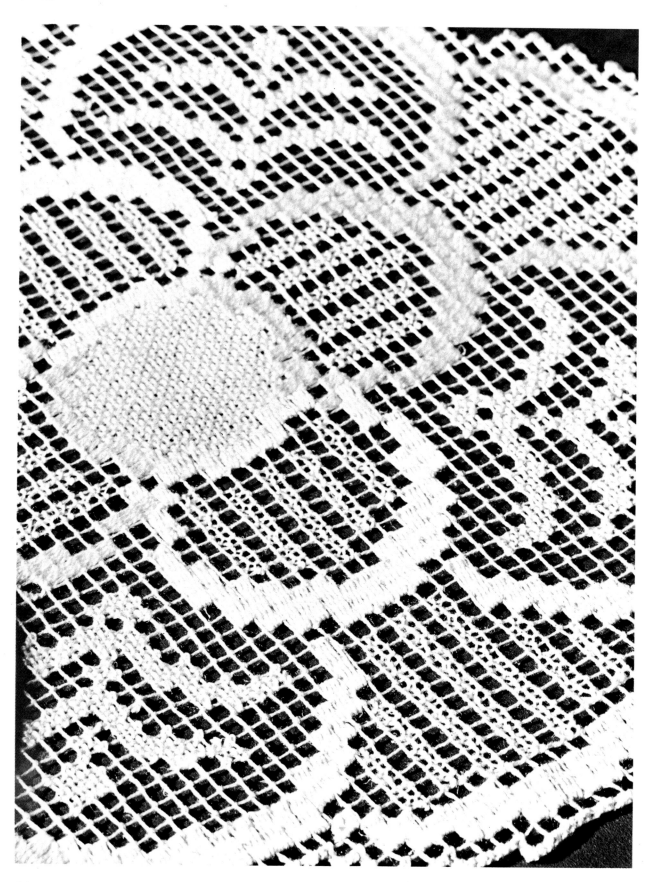

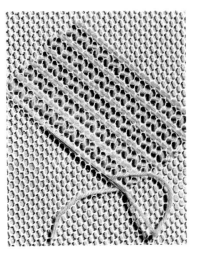

Decorative fillings

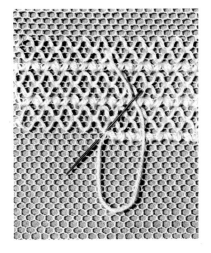

Compound

With the hexagons of tulle horizontal, work two rows of staggered horizontal wavy stitch. Then work one row of oblique stitches, sloping in alterate directions, each covering one mesh of tulle. Work each oblique stitch twice over to give a double thickness of thread.

Cross

This is worked in the same way as it would be embroidered on fabric. First make a row of diagonal stitches from left to right, then return to complete cross with a second row from right to left.

Flower mat, combining linen stitch, darning stitch and loopy filling on net

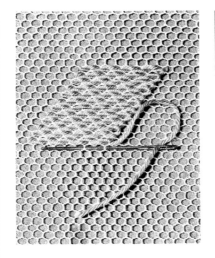

Darning

Work backwards and forwards, passing thread alternately over and under the meshes until the area is complete. Always work two rows of thread in the same meshes so that the return rows fill in the gaps left by the first rows.

Double band

This is worked in two parts. First make parallel lines of back stitches, making each one over two meshes of tulle and spacing rows one mesh a part. Next, run an in and out thread over every other row of back stitches, working from left to right and then returning from right to left on the same row.

Diagonal patterned

Rows of diagonal running stitch, worked double, are alternated with zigzag rows, worked between two diagonal lines of meshes as shown.

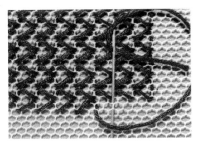

Fishbone

Working over three rows of meshes and from left to right, make a row of stitches which slant from left to right by inserting needle into one hole in first row, taking it down vertically and coming out through the mesh in third row. Miss the next vertical row of meshes before making next stitch in the same way. Work a second row from right to left so that stitches slope in the opposite direction.

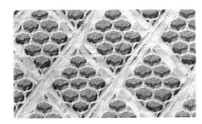

Grating

This consists of diagonal lines

83

E

which cross to form a diamond pattern. Each diagonal is formed by two rows of adjacent running stitch.

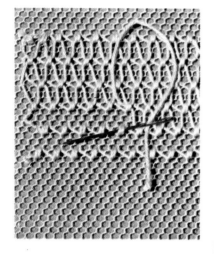

Honeycomb
This is worked in two parts. First, work lines of vertical stitches over one mesh of tulle leaving two or three meshes between the lines. Next, run a second thread in and out of these stitches, alternating rows as shown to form the honeycomb pattern.

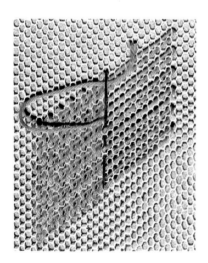

Linen
Another quick way of filling large areas. Simply work rows of running stitch, diagonally or vertically and then cross them with horizontal rows of running stitch.

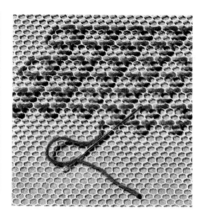

Ring
Working horizontally from right to left, begin by taking the thread over one and under one thread of tulle and thereafter take thread over one thread of tulle, under one, over one and under one. Then, working in an anticlockwise direction outline in running stitch the mesh hole in the row immediately below. The second row is worked three rows of meshes down, the rings worked in a clockwise direction and staggered one hole to the left of those in row above.

Running stitch (interlaced)
First row of running stitch is worked over as many threads as required. Work second row in waves of the same dimensions, alternating and interlacing with first row. At the end of each row make a curved line of running stitch down the side.

Running stitch (staggered)
Work running stitch with a double thread, staggering the stitches by moving one thread along on each row, giving the effect of rows of parallel diagonal lines.

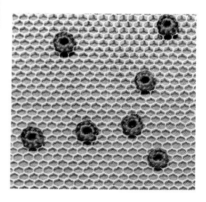

Spot
Work a thread in running stitch round one mesh hole and then work buttonhole stitch over it to form a ring.

Star
These are worked by making six

stitches over two or more threads of tulle, all meeting in a single mesh in the centre. Secure ends of thread by darning them in round centre mesh on back of work.

Threaded
For first row start at right hand side, bringing thread through a mesh hole from back. Take thread down, missing one row of meshes and insert needle one hole to right of first mesh to form a diagonal line. Take needle behind mesh to the left and come out two holes along. Work a back stitch over mesh hole missed, bringing needle out at same place as last time. Take thread back up to first hole thus forming a diagonal line sloping to the right. Continue working back stitches over horizontal meshes linked by diagonal lines as shown.

Second row is worked by passing needle horizontally under two meshes taking thread down over two rows of meshes and one hole diagonally to left, under two horizontal meshes and back up to one hole diagonally to left. These two rows are worked alternately to form pattern.

Wavy
Turn tulle so that hexagons are vertical. Work diagonally, taking one thread of tulle above and one below, missing a hole in between

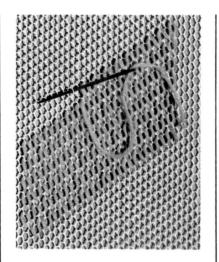

and picking up one thread with each stitch. Subsequent rows are worked by picking up threads missed in previous row. A gentler wavy line can be made by leaving more threads between stitches.

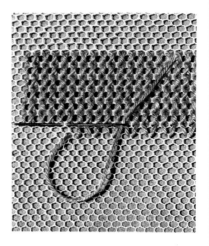

Wavy (double)
With the hexagons horizontal, work a horizontal row of stitches as for wavy stitch, from right to left. Complete row from left to right by working over the same threads but picking up the threads left by the first stage of row, to make a crossed stitch.

Edgings

Buttonhole stitch
Pad edge with a simple running stitch, following outline of the shape. Embroider over it with

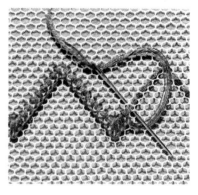

one buttonhole stitch for each mesh of tulle. Work in same way along a straight edge.

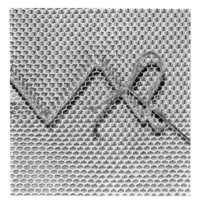

Darning stitch
Secure thread to one mesh of tulle, working from left to right. Hold thread with thumb of left hand. Thread needle through one hole of tulle to the right, pushing it upwards under top thread of mesh being covered. Leaving thread slack, move needle down under lower thread of mesh being covered and over the looped thread. Remove the left thumb from thread and pull thread

E

tight. This gives the effect of darning stitch with a small oblique stitch above it. One stitch is worked into each mesh. (If thread is thin, work two or three stitches into each mesh). Stitch can be worked on the straight or in a zigzag as shown. Once edging stitch and any embroidery which is to be worked as a border is completed, trim off surplus tulle with a small pair of pointed scissors, close to embroidery.

Enlarging or reducing a design

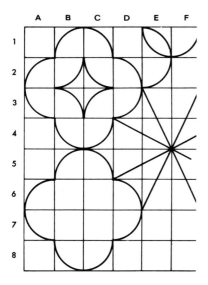

First trace outline of the design on to tracing paper. Carefully transfer tracing to graph or small squared paper. Draw a rectangle round the tracing. Draw a diagonal through the rectangle. Extend two adjacent sides of the rectangle to the final size required, then draw lines at right angles from the ends of the extended sides to meet at the diagonal. If it confuses you to have the rectangles inside one another, draw the larger to one side of the smaller one.

Count the total number of squares in small rectangle and divide larger rectangle into the same number of squares to form a grid. Draw this in ink. Now, in pencil, carefully copy the design on to the larger grid. It will help if you make tiny marks on each square where lines of the design cross it, then join up these marks. To reduce a design, use the same method in reverse.

Symmetrical drawing
In a design of this nature all you have to do is to draw out one quarter section. Divide a square of paper large enough to cover the whole motif into four equal quarters by folding it in half and then in half again. Open out paper. With soft pencil mark out the top right hand quarter of the motif. Fold paper back along vertical fold and trace round outline of motif with dressmaker's tracing wheel or point of compass, so that it makes an impression on the other side. Go over this with pencil. Fold paper in half horizontally and repeat process to obtain complete motif. Go over whole outline with sharp pencil.

Eyelets

Oval
Work a line of running stitches round outline of eyelet. Trim fabric back to running stitches

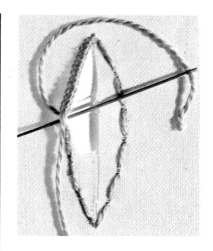

and work overcasting all round, covering running stitches and cut edge. For a more raised effect lay a thread round eyelet before overcasting.

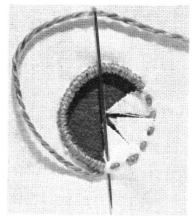

Round
Make a small hole in the fabric with an embroidery stiletto, lay a thread round the edge and cover with overcasting as for oval eyelet. For larger eyelets, work a line of tiny running stitches round the edge, trim fabric back and overcast edge as illustrated.

F

Faggot stitch

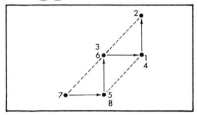

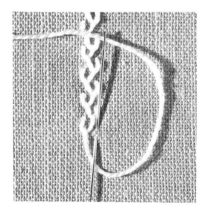

This is a drawn fabric stitch (not to be confused with drawn thread). In drawn fabric work the material is left intact but threads are pulled apart or drawn together by stitchery so that the holes left form a variety of patterns. It should be worked on light, even-weave fabric and can be used as a line stitch, in vertical rows or as a filling. Work diagonally downwards from right to left following numbered diagram. Dotted lines indicate wrong side of work. If you begin the second row with a horizontal stitch, squares will be formed, the stitches being made in the holes of the previous row.

Feather stitch

Work from right to left. Bring needle through above centre line of design. Take a small stitch to the left, below the line, catching the thread under the point of the needle. Continue making a series of stitches above and below the central line, catching thread under needle each time. The result is parallel lines of stitches linked by a zigzag line.

Double feather stitch

Work as for feather stitch, but take two stitches in each direction instead of one.

Fishbone stitch

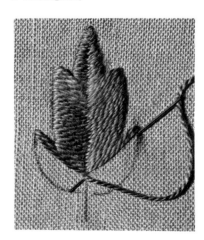

This can be used as a filling or a joining stitch and can be worked open or closed. Bring needle out at left side and insert it sloping down just past centre line. Bring out on right side opposite where you put it in on first side. Continue, taking care to insert needle in centre just past end of last stitch. This gives the plaited effect down the middle which is ideal for marking the veining of leaves.

French knot

Bring needle through to right side of fabric in required position. Take the working thread in your left hand and wind it twice round needle. Then, still holding thread firmly in left hand, insert it close to where it first emerged. Pull needle through to back and secure knot, or bring needle up in position for next stitch. Each stitch should resemble a bead. Use a thick needle with a small eye so it passes through the coiled thread easily.

You can build up a rich border by working rows of evenly spaced French knots in complementary colours.

G

Gathers

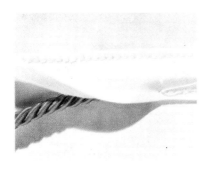

Corded
Cord can be used to form gathers, it is threaded through a casing and then pulled up to the required size. A backing strip of fabric is required, this is cut on the straight grain and its width is that of cord, plus hems, and length that of fabric to be gathered. Pin it to the wrong side under cording position. Tack. Mark two parallel lines for each cord, spaced so that it can be inserted easily Machine stitch one side, insert cord, then stitch other edge. If cord is to be fastened off in centre it should be taken to wrong side by threading through an eyelet, the end is doubled back on itself and sewn firmly to casing lining.

Secured with tape
Cut a strip of tape or straight fabric the length of material after gathering, wide enough to cover the lines of stitching, plus small hems if necessary. Position strip over gathers on wrong side and secure with small stitches.

Gold embroidery

Varieties of threads
Japanese gold: a core of fine silk floss over which finely beaten and cut gold is coiled.
Passing gold thread: this contains a high proportion of gold and has a soft smooth appearance.
Admiralty quality: less expensive but inclined to tarnish.
Synthetic gold thread: even surfaced with a hard shine.
Gold purl: in various thicknesses, this looks like fine metal spring coil.
Coloured embroidery threads can be used for contrast and Maltese silk is recommended for couching. It is essential that a frame is used. Fabric must be held taut in order to support the threads in smooth lines and avoid puckering.

Applied thread
Make a foundation strip of cardboard, painted yellow and punch little holes along the edge. Glue cardboard lightly to fabric and secure with tiny stitches through holes. Wind gold thread on to a roll of felt to prevent kinking. Apply over cardboard, fastening with tiny cross stitches at edges. To finish off ends when work is completed, use a no.18 chenille

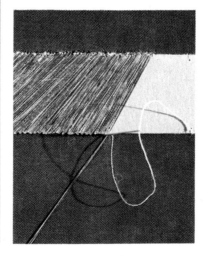

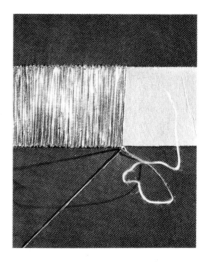

needle, insert point into fabric where metal thread is to go through, thread 2.5cm (1in) of metal through eye of needle and quickly pull through fabric. Trim ends and oversew to backing fabric with two or three stitches.

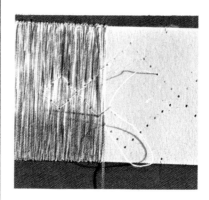

With central design
Prepare cardboard on which design is drawn, punching out outline of design. Glue cardboard to fabric and secure edges as before. Then apply gold thread, stitching it along the outline of the design as well as at the edges.

Couching
This is the method most often used in gold embroidery. Work with two lengths of fine gold thread for both single lines and solid areas. Drag a length of Maltese silk once through a block of beeswax to strengthen it against the friction of the metal threads. Using a no.1

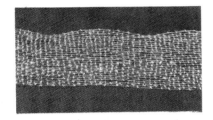

crewel needle, first make a knot at end of silk and then work one small back stitch on design line. Hold the gold threads together in position, leaving about 2.5cm (1in) free, to be worked through fabric later. Work two couching stitches over gold thread, stitching through the same hole in fabric and continue along length of gold thread working single couching stitches about 0.5cm ($\frac{1}{4}$in) apart. Stop about 0.5cm ($\frac{1}{4}$in) from end of design line and make two couching stitches as at beginning and finish with two back stitches. Leave short end to be finished as with applied thread. When a large area of couching is to be worked, instead of cutting both ends of threads on each row, one of the two threads is brought back on the second row with a new single thread. A double stitch is needed on the turn and a hidden double stitch worked to hold new thread in place.

Padded
On shape to be worked build up a thickly padded foundation, first with interwoven running stitches using several strands of silk thread, then covered with satin stitch. Apply the gold thread over this. Padded areas can also be produced with gold kid or other contrasting non-fraying materials, built up underneath with layers of felt and secured with small stitches round edges.

G

Various qualities of gold thread, couched down in different directions have been used here to give a glowing three dimensional effect.

H

Hairpin crochet

Hairpin crochet A head
This consists of long strips joined together to form the finished article. Patterns can be varied in the centre knot between each loop and the way in which completed strips are joined. It is worked on a hairpin frame consisting of two lightweight rods connected at top and bottom by plastic bars. By slotting the rods into different positions on the bars the width can be altered. It is best to work with both end bars on the rods, although the illustrations show the top bar removed. Without the top bar the loops tend to pull the rods together and tension on the finished strip will not be even.

Double crochet

Make a slip knot in yarn and take top bar off until you have placed slip knot on right hand rod. Replace bar. Draw loop out so that knot is exactly central between bars. Hold yarn behind left rod with index finger and thumb of left hand and turn frame towards you from right to left until right hand rod has reversed to left side (1).
Yarn will now pass round other rod and should be held again by left hand behind left hand rod. *Insert crochet hook through loop and draw a single thread through so that there are two loops on crochet hook (2), yarn round hook and draw through both loops to complete one double crochet. Keeping loop on hook, pass hook through to back of frame and turn frame towards you from right to left as before (3). Repeat from*, turning frame after each stitch. Frame is always turned the same way. When frame becomes full of completed loops, remove bottom bar and slip most of the loops off the frame. Replace bar and continue on remaining loops as

before until strip is required length. To finish off, break yarn and draw through last double crochet.

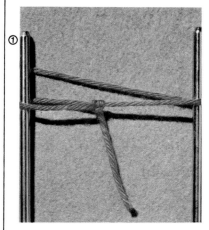

The loop after turning the frame once.

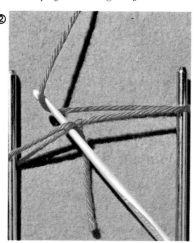

Drawing the first loop through with a crochet hook

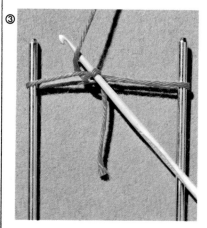

Completing the first stage of the centre stitch

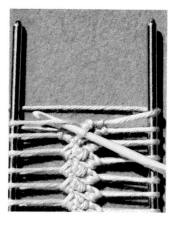

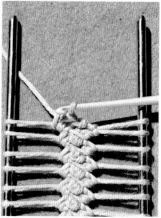

Double double crochet

Work as for double crochet, working two double crochet instead of one by making the first into the loop as before and the second under both threads of loop.

Double crochet on two threads

Work as for double double crochet

90

but make both first and second double crochet under both threads of loop.

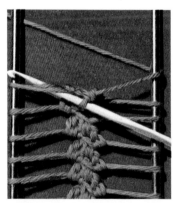

Double crochet with treble on two threads
Work as for double double crochet on two threads, making one double crochet under both threads of loop and then putting yarn round hook and working one treble under both threads of loop.

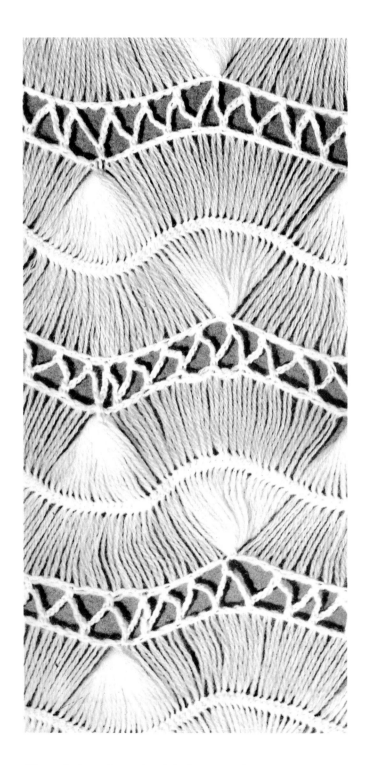

The methods used to anchor hairpin crochet stitches as they are made can vary, but it is the joining of the loops that gives each design its originality. The working instructions for the delicate and airy fan shaped grouping here are given on the following page.

H

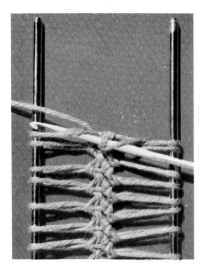

Treble crochet on two threads
Work as for double with treble crochet, making both stitches treble and working them both under two threads of the loop.

Joining strips with crochet hook
Place the two strips together horizontally. Using crochet hook, lift one of the loops from first strip and one from second. Draw second loop through first then pick up second loop of first strip. Draw this through loop on hook, then pick up second loop from second strip and draw loop through. Continue in this way along strips until they are joined together. Make sure that final stitch is securely sewn to prevent unravelling.

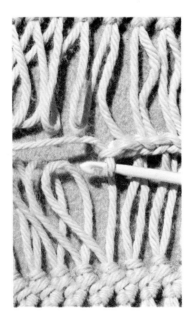

Joining strips with chain stitch
Place two strips together horizontally and work from right to left. Make a slip knot and place on crochet hook. * Insert hook through first loop of first strip and first loop of second strip, yarn round hook and draw through. Repeat from * until all the loops are joined, then finish off thread by drawing it through last stitch.

Fan shaped grouping
Work 3 strips of hairpin crochet using dc on 2 threads. Before joining the strips, work 1 row dc along each side as follows:
1st side * Work 1dc into group of 20 loops, work 1dc into each of next 20 loops, rep from * to end.
2nd side * Work 1dc into each of next 20 loops, work 1dc into group of next 20 loops, rep from * to end.
The strips will now be curved instead of straight and are ready to join together with crochet.
Join yarn to first st at right side of first strip with ss. Work 5ch, work 1dc into 2nd st of left side of 2nd strip, * 5ch, 1dc into 3rd st from last st on 1st strip, 5ch, 1dc, into 3rd st from last st on 2nd strip, rep from * until strips are joined together. Other strips are joined in same way.

Hems

Hems can be decorative as well as practical As shown in the selection below, some them effectively combine both virtues.

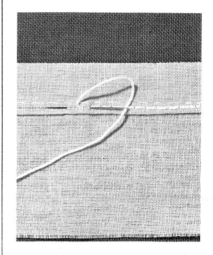

Back stitched
Very strong, therefore useful for household linen. Turn raw edge 1cm ($\frac{3}{8}$in) to wrong side and crease. Make second turn to wrong side the desired depth. Pin and tack. On wrong side, carefully withdraw one thread of the fabric, 2 or 3mm ($\frac{1}{8}$in) from fold. Along this drawn thread line work a line of back stitching to secure hem.

Doubled machined
Generally used for blouses and men's shirts. First make a single machine stitched hem. Then fold fabric a second time on wrong side to enclose first hem, tack and machine stitch.

False

Used for straight hems where there is insufficient fabric for a hem or to add more length. Can also be used decoratively. Cut a strip on the straight grain of hem fabric, 6.5 to 7.5cm (2½ to 3in) wide, plus turnings to length required. Place strip to garment, right sides together, placing strip 0.5cm (¼in) below raw edge. Pin, tack and sew. Remove tacking. Turn hem to wrong side, turn under raw edge and hem stitch into position.

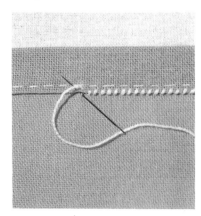

Hand hemmed

Turn under and tack hem which is secured with hemming stitched from right to left. Pick up one thread of fabric, insert needle diagonally into hem, picking up one thread. Continue, picking up one thread alternately from fabric and hem, evenly spacing stitches with a few threads between each one.

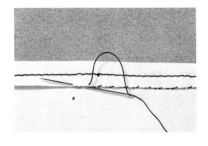

Machined and hemmed

Article should first be machine stitched about 1.5cm (⅝in) from edge. Then fold under fabric to form narrow hem and stitch by hand, using machine stitching as a guide.

Over a seam

Turn up hem, marking point where it will lie over seam. Snip seam at this point and press open so that it lies flat under hem. Then stitch hem in normal way.

Rolled

Used for linen, handkerchiefs, fine fabrics. Roll hem between thumb and first finger of left hand, moistening fingers slightly. Stitch hem, picking up only one thread of fabric being hemmed.

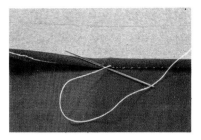

Rolled (strengthened)

Used for linen and fine fabrics that are likely to fray. Make a line of machine stitching close to edge to strengthen it. Then roll hem narrowly to conceal machine stitching and raw edge and stitch, picking up only one thread of fabric being hemmed.

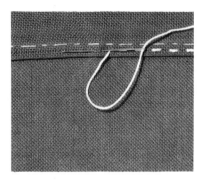

Running stitched

Used for light articles. Fold and prepare hem as required, then secure with a line of little running stitches made one or two threads above folded edge.

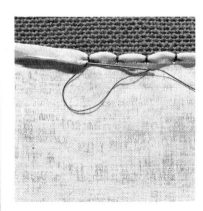

Shell

A decorative hem for fine fabrics, it can be worked in a contrasting thread. First, roll hem edge to

H

depth required. Then, for shell edging, make two stitches over hem, slip needle along for width of shell and then work next two stitches over hem.

Shell (gathered)

A pretty edging, suitable for very light fabrics. First make a narrow, hand stitched hem. Then, on right side of fabric, work a zigzag line of tiny running stitches. Draw up to form gathered shell edge.

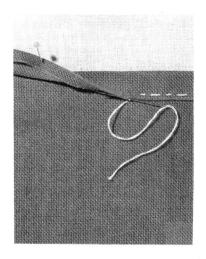

Slip stitched

Turn under and tack hem, about 1cm ($\frac{3}{8}$in) from folded edge. When stitching, insert needle in fold of hem, bring out a few threads along and then pick up one thread of fabric being hemmed, working from right to left.

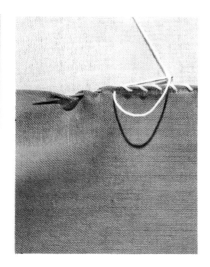

Whipped

Used for fine fabrics, neatening lace. Worked on right side. Roll narrow hem. Insert needle, taking it from back to front, back to front, over rolled edge. Pull thread through and continue.

Herringbone stitch

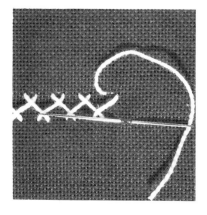

Work from left to right. Bring needle through below centre line of design. Insert needle above this line to the right, taking a small stitch to the left. Then insert needle below the line a little to the right, taking a small stitch towards the left, making sure that needle comes up in line with previous stitch. Herringbone stitch looks best worked very evenly so that the small stitches and spaces between them are of equal size.

Holbein or double running stitch

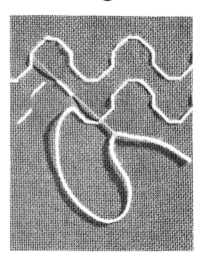

An evenly woven fabric must be used as this stitch must be worked on the counted thread. It is worked in two stages, a first row of running stitch and then a second row filling the spaces left by the first.

Hook and eye

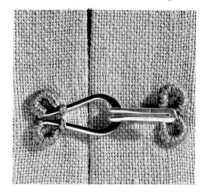

Sew eye on back edge of garment, hook on front. Loop of eye should extend over edge about 2mm ($\frac{1}{16}$in). Hand sew over sides of loop and through each ring separately taking care that stitches do not come through to right side of garment. Set the hook back about 0.5cm ($\frac{3}{16}$in). Stitch under hook, over double wire and through each ring separately.

Holbein stitch, shown here on its own, is frequently combined with cross stitch in Assisi embroidery. It can be worked in pearl cotton, stranded cotton or embroidery cotton on even-weave fabric.

Interlaced band

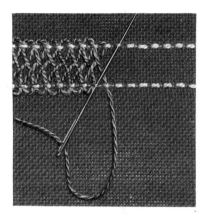

A border stitch in which the thread is mostly on the surface of the fabric. It can be worked in one colour or two different textured threads can be used. First work two parallel rows of back stitch, the width of the border apart. The second thread is laced between these two lines but the needle does not enter the fabric underneath.

Interlacing stitch

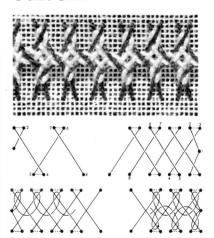

The finished pattern should be tightly knotted and compact, a heavy twisted thread will give the best result. Work in four rows, the first and the third from left to right and the second and fourth

I

from right to left, following diagrams. When the second line of herringboning is completed, the threads interweave regularly, alternately over and under each other. For the final interlacement the thread is brought through to the surface at left hand end of band. It is then taken in a series of loops, in and out of the upper half of the herringbone foundation. At the end of the line, to complete the band, the thread encircles the crossed lines in the centre and then begins a second series of continuous loops, twisted in and out of the foundation threads, this time it must also interlace correctly with the upper series of loops.

Irish crochet lace

Nets

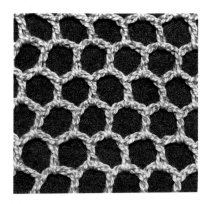

Honeycomb pattern net
This is the background on to which traditional motifs such as shamrock, roses and leaves are then sewn.
Make a chain divisible by 4, plus 11.
1st row Into 10th ch from hook work 1tr, * 4ch, miss 3ch, 1tr into next ch, rep from * to end. Turn.
2nd row 8ch, 1tr into first 4ch loop of previous row, *4ch, 1tr into next 4ch loop, rep from * to end. Turn. The 2nd row forms pattern and·is repeated throughout.

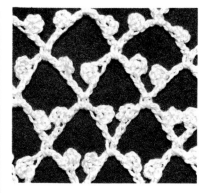

Diamond picot pattern net
Make a chain divisible by 7, plus 2.
1st row Into 2nd ch from hook work 1dc, *2ch, make 5ch and ss into first of these 5ch to form picot, 3ch, 1 picot, 2ch, miss 6ch, 1dc into next ch, rep from * to end. Turn.
2nd row 2ch, 1 picot, 3ch, 1 picot, 2ch, 1dc into 3ch loop between picots of previous row, *2ch, 1 picot, 3ch, 1 picot, 2ch 1dc into next 3ch loop, rep from * to end. Turn.
The 2nd row forms pattern and is repeated throughout.

Shamrock pattern net
Make a loose chain divisible by 5.
1st row *Ss into 5th ch from hook to form picot, 7ch, ss into 5th ch from hook to form 2nd picot, close the shamrock by working 1ss into bottom of first picot, miss 4ch, 1dc into next ch, 8ch, rep from * ending 1dc in last ch. Turn.
2nd row 11ch, work 1ss into 2ch space between picots of previous row, 4ch, 1ss into same 2ch space, * 8ch, 1ss into 5th ch from hook, 7ch, 1ss into 5th ch from hook, 1ss into bottom of first picot, 3ch, 1ss into 2ch space of next 2 picot group, 4ch, 1ss into same 2ch space, rep from * to end. Turn.
The 2nd row forms pattern and is repeated throughout, ending with 1dc into 3rd ch of 11 turning chain.

Motifs

Figure of eight
The picture shows two chain rings being closed into a figure of eight to form the basis of a frog fastening or petal shape. Any number of rings may be joined in this way.
Work 10ch and join into a ring with a dc into 1st ch.
Work 10 more ch to form 2nd ring and join with a ss into 1st ch of first ring. Fasten off.

Five ring motif
Work 10ch and join into a ring with a ss into 1st ch.
1st round Work 18 dc into ring. Join with a ss to 1st dc.
2nd round Work 1dc into each of

This superb bedspread shows how Irish lace motifs combine for their full effect. A project of this size could become a family heirloom.

I

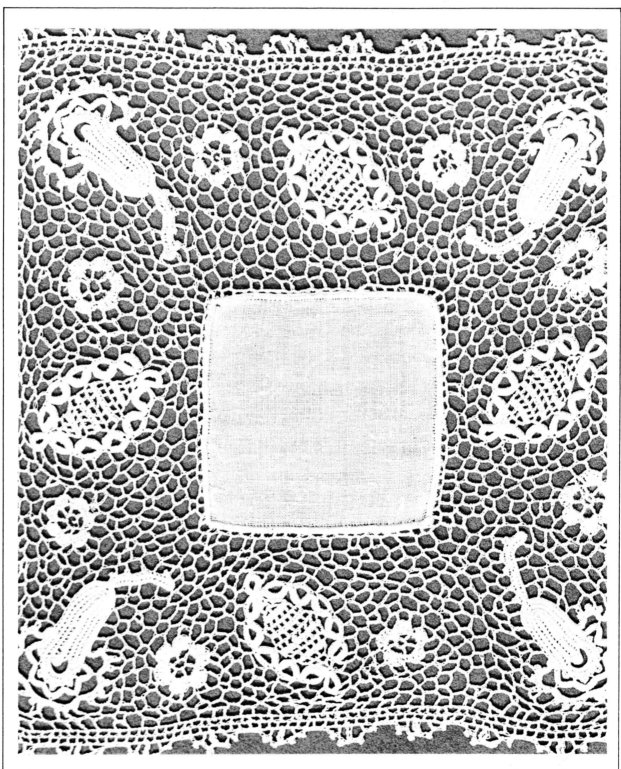

An Irish crochet table centre worked round a linen square with the motifs forming an integral part of the background. An equally pretty effect can be obtained by making the motifs separately and stitching them on to the background using the tiniest possible stitches.

next 3dc picking up back loops only, * 8ch, join into a ring with a ss into 1st ch, work 12dc into ring just formed, 1dc into each of next 3dc in main ring, picking up back loops only, rep from * 4 times more, (5 loops).

Work 10ch to form stem, turn, 1dc into 2nd ch from hook, 1dc into each of next 8ch. Join to next dc in main ring with a ss. Fasten off.

Rose

Work 5ch. Join with a ss to 1st ch to form circle.

1st round 2ch to count as 1dc, * 1ch 1dc into circle, rep from * 4 times more, 1ch. Join with a ss to 2nd of first 2ch.

2nd round 3ch to count as first tr into 1ch sp, 1dc into dc, * 3tr into next 1ch sp, 1dc into dc, rep from * 4 times more. Join with a ss to 3rd of first 3ch.

3rd round *3ch, 1dc round back stem of dc in previous round, rep from * to end.

4th round 3ch to count as 1tr, 4tr into 3ch sp, 1dc into dc, *5tr into 3ch sp, 1dc into dc, rep from * 4 times. Join with a ss to 3rd of first 3ch. Fasten off.

Series of rings

* Work 10ch and join into a ring with a ss into 1st ch.
Work 20dc into this ring and join with a ss to 1st dc, rep from * to

form required number of rings. Fasten off. Picture shows 1st dc being made into 2nd ring.

Shamrock motif

* Work 12ch and join into a ring with a ss into 1st ch.
Work 18dc into this ring and join with a ss into 1st dc, rep from * twice more joining each ring with a ss to base of previous ring. Fasten off. Make 12ch, work 1dc into 2nd ch from hook, then 1dc into each ch to end, to form stem. Join stem to base of rings with a ss. Fasten off.

Wheel motif

Work 4ch and join into a ring with a ss into 1st ch.

1st round 4ch (work 1tr, 1ch) into ring 11 times. Join with a ss into 3rd of first 4ch.

2nd round 1ch, work 3dc into

each 1ch loop between tr on previous round. Join with a ss into first 1ch.

3rd round *5ch, join with a ss to 1st ch to form picot, 1dc into each of next 3dc, rep from * 11 times more. Join with a ss to base of 1st picot. Fasten off.

Japanese painting

Stylized embroidery worked mainly in satin stitch. The motifs are divided into clearly separated sections and worked with paler shades towards the outside deepening in colour towards the centre.

K

Knitting
Casting on

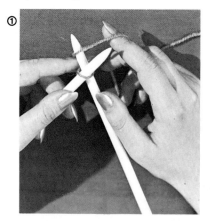

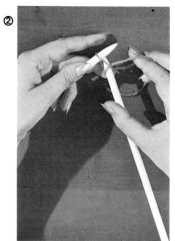

Using two needles

Make a slip loop in yarn, at least 7.3cm (3in) from end. Slip this loop on to left hand knitting needle.

(1) Insert right hand needle into loop holding yarn in right hand and wind yarn under and over the needle.

(2) Draw the new loop through first loop on left hand needle thus forming a second loop. Pass newly made loop on to left hand needle.

(3) Place point of right hand needle between two loops on left hand needle and wind yarn under and over the right hand needle point and draw this new loop through between the two stitches on left hand needle. Slip this loop on to left hand needle.

Repeat step 3 between last 2 stitches on left hand needle until required number of stitches have been cast on.

Using one needle (simple method)

Make a slip loop in yarn about 1 metre (yard) from end. (This length varies with number of stitches to be cast on—1 metre (yard) will cast on about one hundred stitches. A guide to the length required is—the width of the piece of knitting to be cast on, multiplied by three).

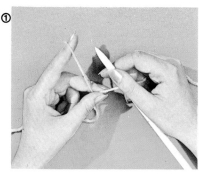

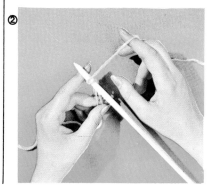

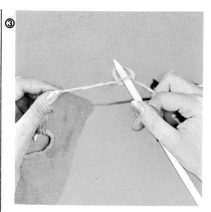

Slip loop on to needle which should be held in right hand.

Working with the short length of yarn in left hand, pass this round left thumb.

Insert point of needle under loop on thumb, and hook forward the long end of yarn from ball.

Wind yarn under and over the needle and draw through loop, leaving stitch on needle.

Tighten stitch on needle, noting that yarn is round thumb ready for next stitch. Repeat last three steps for required number of stitches.

Using one needle (chain method)

Measure off a length of yarn about twice the length of the cast-on required, then make a slip loop at this point and slip the loop on to the needle. Keep the loose end of the yarn in the left hand and the yarn from the ball in the right hand.

Take the yarn in the left hand over the needle as in picture 1 and hold it in place with the first finger. Take the yarn in the right

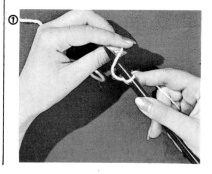

K

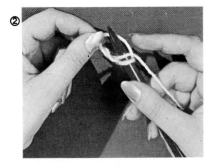

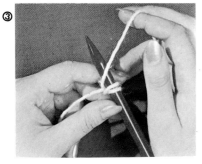

hand round the needle as if to knit a stitch, then lift the left hand loop over the stitch—one stitch has now been cast on. Continue in this way for the length required.

Double

When a less elastic cast on edge is required this method is suitable.

Use a short length of contrasting yarn for casting on. This does not become part of finished work. Using the one needle method, cast

on half number of stitches required.

Using yarn in which garment is to be made, begin with a knit row and work 6 rows of stocking stitch, or required number of rows to give correct depth of hem casing.

Slip the first row of loops which show in the contrast yarn on to a spare needle and unpick contrast yarn.

Fold work in half, holding spare needle behind the other needle and work both sets of stitches on to one needle as follows: * K1 from front needle, P1 from back needle, rep from * until all stitches are on one needle. Continue in rib for required length.

Invisible

Using a contrast yarn, which is later removed, and one needle method, cast on half the number of stitches required, plus one. Now using correct yarn for the garment, begin ribbing.

1st row K1, *yfwd, K1, rep from * to end.

2nd row K1, *yfwd, sl 1, ybk, K1, rep from * to end.

3rd row Sl 1, *ybk, K1, yfwd, sl 1, rep from * to end.

Rep 2nd and 3rd rows once more.

6th row K1, *P1, K1, rep from *

to end.

7th row P1, *K1, P1, rep from * to end.

Continue in rib for the required length. Unpick contrast yarn. The ribs should appear to run right round the edge.

Tubular

There are two methods of working. However many needles are being used (5 or 6 may be required for a large sweater) one is used for knitting and the total number of stitches is divided between the remaining needles. You can either cast on the number of stitches required on the first needle, then proceed to the second and so on, or you can cast on the total number on to one needle and then slip them on to the other needles This

101

K

method is perhaps the easier and is less likely to cause the cast on edge to become twisted.

Form the needles into a circle and slip the spare needle into the first stitch on the first needle. If you now knit this stitch, taking the yarn directly to it from the last stitch, the circle you require is formed. Continue to knit all the stitches on the first needle. Once the needle is free of stitches, knit along the second needle. Continue in this way.

Basic stitches

Knit

Take the needle with the cast-on stitches in your left hand and the other needle in your right hand. Insert right hand needle point through first stitch on left hand needle from front to back.

Keeping yarn away from you behind the needles, pass yarn round the point of the right hand needle so that you form a loop.

Draw this loop through the stitch on the left hand needle, so forming a new loop on the right hand needle.

Allow the stitch on the left hand needle to slip off.

Repeat this action until you have drawn loops through all the stitches on the left hand to the right hand needle.

To work the next row, change the needle holding the stitches to your left hand and the free needle to your right hand and work this row exactly the same way as the first one.

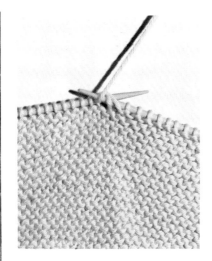

Purl

Take the needle with the cast on stitches in your left hand and the other needle in your right hand. Insert right hand needle point through first stitch on left hand needle from back to front.

Keeping yarn towards you in front of the needles, pass yarn round point of right hand needle to form a loop.

Draw this loop through the stitch on left hand needle, thus forming a new loop on right hand needle. Allow stitch on left hand needle to slip off.

Repeat this action with the next stitch, until you have drawn loops through all the stitches on the left hand needle and passed them on to the right hand needle. You have now purled one row. Change the needles and work other rows in same way

Garter

This is formed by working every row in the same stitch, either knit

or purl. However, instructions for garter stitch intend you to knit every row, because this produces a smoother fabric.

Stocking

This is made by knitting one row and purling the next, alternately. The knit side of the work is usually called the right side. If the pattern uses the purl side as the right side this is called reversed stocking stitch.

Aran knitting

Aran diamond

Cast on 17 sts.

1st row P7, K1, P1, K1, P7.

2nd row K7, P1, K1, P1, K7.

3rd row P6, sl next st to cable needle and leave at back of work,

Matinée set, worked in twisted garter stitch and trimmed with frilling

K

K1, then P1 from cable needle, — called C2B —, K1, sl next st to cable needle and leave at front of work, P1, then K1 from cable needle, — called C2F —, P6.

4th row K6, (P1, K1) twice, P1, K6.

5th row P5, C2B, K1, P1, K1, C2F, P5.

6th row K5, (P1, K1) 3 times, P1, K5.

7th row P4, C2B, (K1, P1) twice, K1, C2F, P4.

8th row K4, (P1, K1) 4 times, P1, K4.

9th row P3, C2B, (K1, P1) 3 times, K1 C2F, P3.

10th row K3, (P1, K1) 5 times, P1, K3.

11th row P2, C2B, (K1, P1) 4 times, K1 C2F, P2.

12th row K2, (P1, K1) 6 times, P1, K2.

13th row P2, C2F, (P1, K1) 4 times, P1, C2B, P2.

14th row As 10th.

15th row P3, C2F, (P1, K1) 3 times, P1, C2B, P3.

16th row As 8th.

17th row P4, C2F, (P1, K1) twice, P1, C2B, P4.

18th row As 6th.

19th row P5, C2F, P1, K1, P1, C2B, P5.

20th row As 4th.

21st row P6, C2F, P1, C2B, P6.

22nd row As 2nd.

23rd row P7, sl next 2 sts to cable needle and leave at front of work, K1, then K1, P1 from cable needle, P7.

24th row K8, P2, K7.

25th row P7, K1, C2F, P7.

26th row As 2nd.

The 3rd to 26th rows form the pattern.

Aran pattern with bobbles

Cast on 29 sts.

1st row K5, P7, K2 make bobble as follows (P1, K1, P1, K1, P1) all into the next st, turn, K5, turn, P5, sl 2nd, 3rd, 4th and 5th sts over the first st — called MB —, K2, P7, K5.

2nd row P5, K7, P2, P into the back of next st, — called PB1 —,

P2, K7, P5.

3rd row K5, P6, sl next st on to cable needle and leave at back of work, K2, then P1 from cable needle, —(called C3B)—, K into back of next st — called KB1 —, sl next 2 sts on to cable needle and leave at front of work, P1, then K2 from cable needle, — called C3F —, P6, K5.

4th row P5, K6, P2, K1, PB1, K1, P2, K6, P5.

5th row K5, P5, C3B, P1, KB1, P1, C3F, P5, K5.

6th row P5, K5, P2, (PB1, K1) twice, PB1, P2, K5, P5.

7th row K2, MB, K2, P4, C3B, (KB1, P1) twice, KB1, C3F, P4, K2, MB, K2.

8th row P5, K4, P2, (K1, PB1) 3 times, K1, P2, K4, P5.

9th row K1, (MB, K1) twice, P3, C3B, (P1, KB1) 3 times, P1, C3F, P3, (K1, MB) twice, K1.

10th row P5, K3, P2, (PB1, K1) 4 times, PB1, P2, K3, P5.

11th row K5, P2, C3B, (KB1, P1) 4 times, KB1, C3F, P2, K5.

12th row P5, K2, P2, (K1, PB1) 5 times, K1, P2, K2, P5.

These 12 rows form the pattern.

Lobster claw stitch

Cast on a number of stitches divisible by 9 plus 2, i.e., 29 stitches.

1st row P2, *K7, P2, repeat from * to end.

2nd row K2, *P7, K2, repeat from * to end.

3rd row P2, *slip 2 sts on to cable needle and hold at back of work, K1 from left hand needle then K2 from cable needle, K1, slip 1 st on to cable needle and

hold at front of work, K2 sts from left hand needle then K1 from cable needle — called Cr7 —, P2, repeat from * to end.

4th row P2, *P7, K2, repeat from * to end.

Repeat these 4 rows 7 times more. Cast off.

Trellis sampler

The sampler is edged with a narrow panel of twisted stitches and is ideal for working in strips, which can then be joined together to make cushions, rugs or bedspreads.

Worked over 58 stitches.

1st row K1, P1, K1 putting yarn twice round needle — called K1y2rn —, K2, P2, K1, P3, *(sl 2 sts on to cable needle and hold at back of work, K2, K2 from cable needle — called C4B —, P4) 4 times, C4B, P3, K1, P2, K1y2rn, K2, P1, K1.

2nd row K2, P2 sl, 1 dropping extra loop and keeping yarn on

A beautifully textured Aran jersey with interesting saddle shoulder line

104

K

WS, K2, P1, K2, (P4, K4) 3 times, P4, K3, P1, K2, P2, sl 1 dropping extra loop and keeping

yarn on WS, K2.

3rd row K1, P1, sl next st on to cable needle and hold at front of work, Kly2rn, K1, K1 from cable needle — called CTw3 —, P2, K1, P2, (sl next st on to cable needle and hold at back of work, K2, P1 from cable needle — called C3PB —, sl next 2 sts on to cable needle and hold at front of work, P1, K2 from cable needle — called C3PF —, P2) 5 times, K1, P2, CTw3, P1, K1.

4th row K2, P2, sl 1, K2, P1, K2, (P2, K2) 10 times, P1 K2, P2, sl 1, K2.

5th row K1, P1, CTw3, P2, K1, P1, (C3PB, P2, C3PF) 5 times, P1, K1, P2, CTw3, P1, K1,

6th row K2, P2, sl 1, K2, P1, K1, (P2, K4, P2) 5 times, K1, P1, K2, P2, sl 1, K2.

7th row K1, P1, CTw3, P2, K1, P1, K2, P4, (sl next 2 sts on to cable needle and hold at front of work, K2, K2 from cable needle — called C4F —, P4) 4 times, K2, P1, K1, P2, CTw3, P1 K1.

8th row K2, P2, sl 1, K2, P1, K1, (P2, K4, P2) 5 times, K1, P1, K2, P2, sl 1, K2.

9th row K1, P1, CTw3, P2, K1, P1, (C3PF, P2, C3PB) 5 times, P1, K1, P2, CTw3, P1, K1.

10th row K2, P2, sl 1, K2, P1, K1, (K1, P2, K1) 10 times, K1,

P1, K2, P2, sl 1, K2.

11th row K1, P1, CTw3, P2, K1, P2, (C3PF, C3PB, P2) 5 times, K1, P2, CTw3, P1, K1.

12th row K2, P2, sl 1, K2, P1, K1, (K2, P4, K2) 5 times, K1, P1, K2, P2, sl 1, K2.

13th row K1, P1, CTw3, P2, K1, P3, (C4B, P4) 4 times, C4B, P3, K1, P2, CTw3, K2, P1, K1.
Rows 2-13 form pattern and are repeated throughout.

Borders, knitted in

These are knitted at the same time as the rest of the work, but in a different stitch. The border illustrated is worked in moss stitch with the main part of the garment in stocking stitch. For a smooth edge, slip the first knit stitch in every row and always end the row with a knit stitch.

Buttonholes

Simple

When buttonhole is to be made as part of the main fabric of a garment, finish at centre front edge. On the next row, work a few stitches to the position for the buttonhole, then cast off the number of stitches needed to take the button and work to end of row. On the following row, work to the cast off stitches in previous row,

turn work and cast on the same number of stitches, turn the work again and continue to end of row. To make the buttonhole look even, always remember to work the stitch immediately after the last cast on stitch fairly tightly.

Tailored

When position for buttonhole is reached, work the stitches required to take the button in a different coloured yarn, then slip these stitches back on to the left hand needle and work them again in the original yarn being used. When work is finished, pull out the different coloured yarn, taking care not to drop the stitches. Complete the buttonhole by threading a length of the correct yarn through these stitches. Oversew or buttonhole stitch round the edges to hold and neaten buttonhole.

K

Vertical

Work until point for buttonhole is reached. On next row work a few stitches to the position for the buttonhole, then work required number of rows over these stitches to take the button. Break off yarn and return to the remaining stitches. Rejoin yarn and work the same number of rows over these stitches, then continue across all the stitches in usual way.

Cable stitch

Simple twist from left to right

Cable designs are based on stitches being moved from one position to another by crossing over each other. When altering the position of more than two stitches it is easier to do so by means of a third needle. For this purpose a

short cable needle is best, if it is not the same thickness as the needles being used, it should be finer, not thicker.

Work a test cable of six knit stitches against a background of purl fabric as follows:

Cast on 24 sts.

1st row P9, K6, P9.

2nd row K9, P6, K9.

Rep 1st and 2nd rows twice more.

7th row P9, slip the next 3 knit stitches on to the cable needle and hold them at back of work; with right hand needle continue to knit the next 3 knit stitches from left hand needle, then knit the 3 stitches from the cable needle, P9.

8th row As 2nd.

Repeat these 8 rows twice more. Cast off. (Abbreviation for this st. is C6B)

Simple twist from right to left

Cast on 24 sts.

1st row P9, K6, P9.

2nd row K9, P6, K9.

3rd row As 1st.

4th row As 2nd.

5th row As 1st.

6th row As 2nd.

7th row P9, slip the next 3 knit stitches on to the cable needle and hold them at the front of the work; with right hand needle continue to knit the next 3 knit stitches from left hand needle, then knit the 3 stitches from the cable needle, P9.

8th row As 2nd

Repeat these 8 rows twice more.

Cast off. (Abbreviation for this st. is 6CF)

Crossed miniature cable

Worked over a number of stitches divisible by 7, plus 3.

1st row P3, *K4, P3, rep from * to end.

2nd row K3, *P4, K3, rep from * to end.

3rd row P3, *(cross 2R) twice, P3, rep from * to end.

4th row As 2nd.

These 4 rows form the pattern and are repeated throughout.

Crossing two stitches to right (cross 2R)

Pass right hand needle in front of first stitch on left hand needle and knit into 2nd stitch. Lift it over 1st stitch and off point of needle. Knit 1st stitch on left hand needle.

Mock cable

Worked over a number of stitches divisible by 5, plus 3.

1st row P3, *K2P3, rep from * to end.

2nd row K3, *P2, K3, rep from * to end.

Rep 1st and 2nd rows once more.

5th row P3, *Tw2B, P3, rep from * to end.

6th row As 2nd.

These 6 rows form pattern and are repeated throughout.

Note: For Tw2B, see Honeycomb.

107

K

3rd row P2, sl next 2 sts on to cable needle and leave at back of work, K2, then K2 from cable needle, — called C4B —, sl next 2 sts on to cable needle and leave at front of work, K2, then K2 from cable needle, — called C4F —, P2.
4th row As 2nd.
5th-8th rows As 1st-4th rows.
9th row As 1st.
10th row As 2nd.
11th row P2, C4F, C4B, P2.
12th row As 2nd.
13th-16th rows As 9th-12th rows.
These 16 rows form the pattern.

Plaited cable
Cast on 13 sts.
1st row P2, K9, P2.
2nd row K2, P9, K2.
3rd row P2, sl next 3 sts on to

cable needle and leave at back of work, K3, then K3 from cable needle — called C6B —, K3, P2.
4th row As 2nd.
5th row As 1st.
6th row As 2nd.
7th row P2, K3, sl next 3 sts on to cable needle and leave at front of work, K3, then K3 from cable needle, — called C6F —, P2.
8th row As 2nd.
These 8 rows form the pattern.

Ribbed cable
Cast on 11 sts.
1st row P2, K into back of next st, — called KB1 —, *P1, KB1, rep from * twice more, P2.
2nd row K2, P into back of next st, — called PB1 —, *K1, PB1, rep from * twice more, K2.
3rd-6th rows Rep the 1st and 2nd rows twice more.
7th row P2, sl the next 3 sts on to cable needle and leave at front of work, (KB1, P1) twice, then KB1, P1, KB1 from cable needle, P2.
8th row As 2nd.
9th-12th rows Rep the 1st and 2nd rows twice more.
These 12 rows form the pattern.

Bright colours are mixed and matched in this eye-catching twinset. The fine stripe in the pullover echoes the colour of the cardigan and the buttons on the cardigan tone with the pullover. Cable stitch is used for both.

Cable rope with row variations
The appearance of the cable is altered very much by the number of rows worked between each twist. Work a sample as follows:
Cast on 24 sts.
1st row P9, K6, P9.
2nd row K9, P6, K9.
Rep 1st and 2nd rows once more.
5th row P9, C6F, P9.
6th row As 2nd.
Repeat 1st and 2nd rows, then 5th and 6th rows once.
Repeat 1st and 2nd rows twice, then 5th and 6th rows once.
Repeat 1st and 2nd rows 6 times, then 5th and 6th rows once.
Repeat 1st and 2nd rows once.
Cast off.

Oxox cable
Cast on 12 sts.
1st row P2, K8, P2.
2nd row K2, P8, K2.

K

Casting off

Two needle method

On a knit row, knit the first two stitches. Then * with left hand needle point, lift first stitch over second stitch, leaving one stitch on right hand needle. Knit the next stitch, repeat from * until all but one stitch have been worked off. Cut the yarn, draw through last stitch and pull stitch tight. On a purl row, each stitch is purled before it is cast off.

With crochet hook

Pick up first and second stitches from left hand needle. Draw second stitch through first. Pick up next stitch and continue in this way to end of row. Fasten off last stitch and yarn left on right.

In rib

To cast off ribbed work, lift each stitch over the next stitch following the pattern of the knitting.

This keeps the casting off as elastic as the rest of the ribbing.

①

②

Invisible

Invisible casting off is useful for finishing neck edging, belts and hems, collars, V-necks and round necks, cuffs, pocket trims and edgings.

When you have reached the required length of the work break yarn, leaving a length at least three times the length of the edge to be cast off and thread this into a bodkin or wool needle. Hold the bodkin in the right hand and the stitches in the left hand, working throughout from right to left along the stitches on the needle. Insert the bodkin in the first two stitches as if to knit them, pulling the yarn through each in turn, leaving both stitches on the left-hand needle.

*First work 2 stitches. Insert bodkin in first stitch as if to knit it, pull yarn through and slip off needle.

Pass bodkin in front of the next stitch as if to purl it and again the following stitch (1). Pull yarn through. Repeat from * (2) until all stitches have been worked. Fasten off.

Worked double

Knit two stitches together. Replace the stitch you have made on left hand needle and knit it together with the next . Continue to end.

Corners

Garter stitch

Cast on required number of sts and mark corner st with coloured thread.

1st row (right side) K to within 2 sts of corner st, K2 tog, K corner st, K2 tog tbl, K to end.

2nd row K to corner st, P corner st, K to end.

Rep these 2 rows until edge is required depth. Cast off still decreasing on either side of corner st.

Moss stitch, (corner and borders)
Cast on an odd number of sts, allowing 10 sts for each side border.

1st row *K1, P1, rep from * to last st, K1.
Rep 1st row 9 times more for lower moss st edge.
11th row (K1, P1) 5 times, K to last 10 sts, (P1, K1) 5 times.
12th row (K1, P1) 5 times, P to last 10 sts (P1, K1) 5 times. Rep 11th and 12th rows until work is required size, less 10 rows. Rep 1st row 10 times more for top moss stitch edge. Cast off.

Stocking stitch
Cast on required number of sts, or pick up sts on wrong side of work. Mark corner st with coloured thread.

1st row (right side) K to corner st, inc 1 by knitting into loop between sts, K corner st, inc 1 as before K to end.
2nd row P to end.
Rep these 2 rows until edge is required depth ending with a 1st row. Cast off P-wise.

Decreasing

Decorative decrease with holes
To decrease towards the right, K to last 6 sts, yfwd, K2 tog, K2 tog,

K2. Next row, P to end (including yfwd of previous row). To decrease towards the left, P to last 6 sts, yrn, P2 tog, P2 tog, P2. Next row, K to end (including yrn of previous row).

In pairs on alternate rows
When decreasing on knit rows of stocking stitch on right hand side of work slip 1, knit 1, pass slipped stitch over (sl 1, K1, psso). These stitches will slant to left. For other end of row use a knit 2 together (K2 tog) decrease. These stitches will slant to the right. When used at opposite ends on alternate rows, they will then give you the inward sloping chain effect shown in the illustration.

Knitting two together
On a knit row, insert point of right hand needle through two stitches instead of one and knit them together in the usual way. This stitch will slant to right and abbreviation is 'K 2 tog'. If the decrease is on a purl row, purl

two stitches together in the same way. Stitch will slant to left and abbreviation is 'P2 tog'.

Simple double decrease
Knitting three stitches together (K 3 tog) gives you a right slanting decrease.
Knitting three stitches together through the back of the loops (K3 tog tbl) gives you a left slanting decrease. A neater form of this left slanting decrease is to slip the first stitch and then the second stitch from left to right hand needles. Knit the next stitch. With left hand needle point, lift both slipped stitches over the knitted stitch.

Twisted decorative
This decrease is accentuated by having been twisted as well as lying in the opposite direction to the line of the seam. It is worked at the end of right side or knit rows for the left hand side and at the end of wrong side or purl rows for the right hand side. Knit to last 6 stitches, pass right hand

K

needle behind first stitch on left hand needle and knit next 2 stitches together through backs of loops, then knit first stitch and slip both stitches off left hand needle. Knit last 3 stitches in usual way. On next row purl to the last 6 stitches, pass right hand needle across front of first stitch on left hand needle and purl next 2 stitches together, then purl the first stitch and slip both stitches off left hand needle. Purl last 3 stitches as usual.

With a slipped stitch

Most commonly used where decreases are paired, one slanting to the left and one to the right as on a raglan sleeve. Slip first stitch on left hand needle on to right hand needle, then knit the next stitch. With point of left hand needle lift the slipped stitch over the knit stitch and off the needle. This stitch will slant to left and abbreviation is 'sl 1, K1, psso'. If decrease is on a purl row, purl two stitches together through back of stitches. Stitch will slant to right and abbreviation is 'P2 tog tbl'.

Dropped stitch, picking up

Insert a crochet hook into the dropped stitch with the knit side of the work facing. Lift the first thread above the stitch on to the hook tip, and hold it in the hook curve as you slowly draw the hook back until the first stitch slips off the tip, leaving the lifted thread as the new stitch. Repeat this until all the threads have been lifted then return the stitch to the needle. If the purl side is the right side lift the stitch on the wrong or knit side.

Edges

Edge stitch

The edges of your work will be neater and therefore more easily made up, if you slip the first stitch and knit the last stitch of each row. This is particularly the case with stocking stitch where row ends tend to be slack. Knitting the last stitch of every row tightens this edge and gives a neat finish.

Leaf edging

Cast on 10 stitches.
1st row K3, (yfwd, K2 tog) twice, bring yarn forward and over the needle, then forward and over the needle again to make 2 sts — called y2rn —, K2 tog, K1.
2nd row K3, P1, K2, (yfwd, K2, tog) twice, K1.
3rd row K3, (yfwd, K2 tog) twice, K1, y2rn, K2 tog, K1.
4th row K3, P1, K3, (yfwd, K2 tog) twice, K1.
5th row K3, (yfwd, K2 tog) twice, K2, y2rn, K2 tog, K1.
6th row K3, P1, K4, (yfwd, K2 tog) twice, K1.
7th row K3, (yfwd, K2 tog) twice, K6.
8th row Cast off 3 sts, K5, (yfwd, K2 tog) twice, K1.
These 8 rows form the pattern.

Fabric stitches

K

Alternated rib and bobble

Cast on a number of stitches divisible by 9, plus 4.

1st row * K4, P2, K1, P2, rep from * to last 4 sts, K4.

2nd row * P4, K2, P1, K2, rep from * to last 4 sts, P4.

3rd row * K4, P2, bobble 1 in K st, P2, rep from * to last 4 sts, K4. (see Small Bobble, p.117)

4th row As 2nd.

These 4 rows form pattern and are repeated throughout.

Begonia

Cast on a number of stitches divisible by 7, plus 2 at each end.

1st row K2, *P2, K2 tog, inc 1, sl 1, K1, bring sl st back on to left hand needle, K1 *. Repeat from * to *, K2.

2nd row P2, *K2, P5 *. Repeat from * to *.

These two rows form pattern.

Broken rib

Cast on a number of stitches divisible by 4, plus 1.

1st row *K2, P1, K1, rep from * to last st, K1.

2nd row *P1, K3, rep from * to last st, P1.

Rep these 2 rows for length required.

Broken vertical rib

Worked over a number of stitches divisible by 6.

1st, 3rd and 5th rows * K3, P1 tbl, K2, rep from * to end.

2nd, 4th and 6th rows * P2, K1 tbl, P3, rep from * to end.

7th, 9th and 11th rows * P1 tbl, K5, rep from * to end.

8th, 10th and 12th rows * P5, K1 tbl, rep from * to end.

These 12 rows form the pattern.

Cluster cushions

These can be worked while knitting is in progress or after completion by threading the yarn several times round a group of two or more stitches. Groups of cushions can be used on either the purl or knit side of stocking stitch. To work them in as part of the fabric, work to position where a cluster is required, slip next 3 stitches on to a cable or spare needle, pass the yarn round these stitches from back to front until cushion is required size, 6 to 8 times should be sufficient, then work the 3 stitches from holder in usual way and continue to position for next cluster. Where a very chunky effect is required, work 2 rows on the 3 stitches before winding yarn round.

Crossed basket weave stitch

Worked over an even number of stitches.

1st row * Holding yarn at back of work, sl 1 purlwise, K next st, yon, lift slipped stitch over both knitted stitch and yon, rep from * to end.

2nd row P.

3rd row K1, work from * as for 1st row to last st, K1.

4th row P.

These 4 rows form the pattern and are repeated throughout.

Diamond quilting pattern

Cast on a number of stitches divisible by 6 plus 2.

1st row K to end.

2nd row P1, P1 winding yarn

K

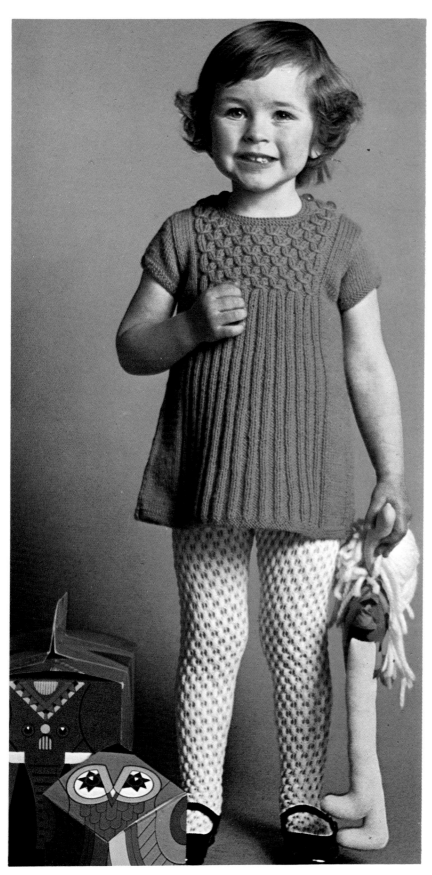

twice round needle, *P4, P2 winding yarn twice round needle for each rep from * to last 6 sts, P4, P1 winding yarn twice round needle, P1.

3rd row K1, sl 1 dropping the extra loop, *K4, sl 2 dropping the extra loops, rep from * to last 6 sts, K4, sl 1 dropping the extra loop, K1.

4th row P1, sl 1, *P4, sl 2, rep from * to last 6 sts, P4, sl 1, P1.

5th row K1, sl 1, *K4, sl 2, rep from * to last 6 sts, K4, sl 1, K1.

6th row As 4th.

7th row K1, *sl next st on to a cable needle and leave at front of work, K2, then K1 from cable needle — called C3F —, sl next 2 sts to a cable needle and leave at back of work, K1, then K2 from cable needle — called C3B —, rep from * to last st, K1.

8th row P3, *P2, winding yarn twice round needle for each, P4, rep from * to last 5 sts, P2 winding yarn twice round needle, P3.

9th row K3, *sl 2 dropping the extra loops, K4, rep from * to last 5 sts, sl 2 dropping the extra loops, K3.

10th row P3, *sl 2, P4, rep from * to last 5 sts, sl 2, P3.

11th row K3, *sl 2, K4, rep from * to last 5 sts, sl 2, K3.

12th row As 10th.

13th row K1, *C3B, C3F, rep from * to last st, K1.

14th row As 2nd.

The 3rd to 14th rows form the pattern.

Diagonal slip stitch pattern
Cast on a number of stitches divisible by 5 plus 2.

1st row P2, *sl 3, P2, rep from * to end.

2nd row P to end.

3rd row P3, *sl 3, P2, rep from * to last 4 sts. sl 3, P1.

4th row As 2nd.

5th row P1, sl 1, *P2, sl 3, rep

Grown-up dress for a little girl has a well-shaped skirt with ribbed front.

K

from * to last 5 sts. P2, sl 2, P1.
6th row As 2nd.
7th row P1, sl 2, *P2, sl 3, rep from * to last 4 sts, P2, sl 1, P1.
8th row As 2nd.
9th row P1, sl 3, *P2, sl 3, rep from * to last 3 sts, P3.
10th row As 2nd.
These 10 rows form the pattern.

Honeycomb
Worked over a number of stitches divisible by 4.
1st row *Tw2B, Tw2F, rep from * to end.
2nd row P.
3rd row *Tw2F, Tw2B, rep from * to end.
4th row P.
These 4 rows form the pattern and are repeated throughout.

Knitted crossed stitches with back twist. Tw2B.
The twist lies to the left. Pass right hand needle behind first stitch on left hand needle, knit into back of next stitch and leave on needle. Then knit into back of first stitch and slip both stitches from left hand to right hand needle.

Knitted crossed stitches with front twist. Tw2F.
The twist lies to the right. Pass right hand needle in front of first stitch on left hand needle and knit next stitch, leaving it on needle. Then knit first stitch and slip both stitches off left hand needle on to right hand needle.

Horizontal rib
Worked over an even number of stitches.
1st row K.
2nd row P.
3rd row *K1, P1, rep from * to end.
4th row K the K sts and P the P sts. These 4 rows form the pattern.

Mock smocking
Cast on a number of stitches divisible by 6 plus 2.
1st row P2, *K4, P2, rep from * to end.
2nd row K2, *P4, K2, rep from * to end.
3rd row P2, *insert needle between 4th and 5th stitches and draw up a loop, K4, then pass the top thread of the loop over these 4 sts, P2, rep from * to end.
4th row As 2nd.
5th row K3, *P2, K4, rep from * to last 5 sts, P2, K3.
6th row P3, *K2, P4, rep from * to last 5 sts, K2, P3.
7th row Insert needle between 3rd and 4th stitches and draw up

a loop, K3, then pass the top thread of the loop over these 3 sts, *P2, insert needle between 4th and 5th stitches and draw up a loop, K4, then pass the top thread of the loop over these 4 sts, rep from * to last 5 sts, P2, insert needle after last st on left hand needle and draw up a loop, K3, then pass the top thread of the loop over these 3 sts.
8th row As 6th.
These 8 rows form the pattern.

Moss stitch
Cast on an odd number of stitches.
1st row K1, * P1, K1, rep from * to end.
Rep this row for length required.

115

K

Plain woven stitch
Worked over an even number of stitches, plus 2 edge stitches.
1st row K.
2nd row K1, * yfwd, sl 1 knit-wise, rep from * to last st, K1.
3rd row K1, * K2 tog tbl thus working together the slipped and the made stitch on previous row, rep from * to last st, K1.
The 2nd and 3rd rows form pattern and are repeated throughout.

Plaited rib
Cast on a number of stitches divisible by 5.
1st row *K2, sl 1 P-wise, yfwd. *Repeat from * to *, K2.
2nd row * P2, K2 tog, repeat from * to end.
These two rows form pattern.

Rice stitch
Cast on a number of stitches

Mock smoking and satin bow ties contrast with simple stocking stitch to make a warm and glamorous bedjacket.

divisible by 2 plus 1.
1st row K to end.
2nd row P1, *K1, P1, repeat from * to end. These two rows form the pattern.

Single rib
Cast on an even number of stitches.
1st row *K1, P1, rep from * to end. Rep this row for length required.

Small bobble
Cast on a number of stitches divisible by 6, plus 5 stitches.
Beginning with a knit row, work 2 rows stocking stitch.
1st row K2 sts, work a bobble by K 5 times into next st, first into the front and then into the back alternately (picture 1) and leaving last st on left hand needle.
Slip st off left hand needle (picture 2) leaving 5 sts on right hand needle. Pass 2nd, 3rd, 4th and 5th sts over first st (picture 3) and off right hand needle to complete bobble, * K5 sts, make a bobble in 6th st as before, rep from * to last

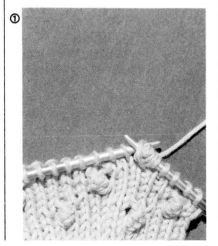

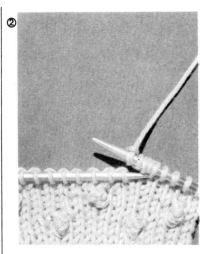

2 sts, K2.
2nd row P to end.
3rd row *K5 sts, make a bobble in next st as before, rep from * to last 5 sts, K5.
4th row P to end.
These 4 rows form pattern and are repeated throughout.

Trellis stitch
Cast on a number of stitches divisible by 6 plus 2.
1st row P3, *K2, P4, rep from * to last 5 sts, K2, P3.
2nd row K3, *P2, K4, rep from * to last 5 sts, P2, K3.
3rd row As 1st.
4th row As 2nd.
5th row P1, *sl next 2 sts on to a cable needle and leave at back of work, K1, then P2 from cable needle — called C3B —, sl next st on to a cable needle and leave

K

at front of work, K1 then P2 from cable needle —, called C3F —, rep from * to last st, P1.

6th row K1, P1, *K4, P2, rep from * to last 6 sts, K4, P1, K1.

7th row P1, K1, *P4, K2, rep from * to last 6 sts, P4, K1, P1.

8th row As 6th.

9th row As 7th.

10th row As 6th.

11th row P1, *C3F, C3B, rep from * to last st, P1.

12th row As 2nd.

These 12 rows form the pattern.

Two colour brioche

Using A cast on a number of stitches divisible by 2, plus 1.

1st row With A K to end.

2nd row As first.

3rd row With B, K1, * K into the loop below the next st—called K1 below —, K1, rep from * to end.

4th row With B K to end.

5th row With A, K2, * K1 below, K1, rep from * to last st, K1.

6th row With A K to end.

The 3rd to 6th rows form the pattern.

Woven herringbone

Worked over an even number of stitches.

1st row K2 tog tbl but drop only

1st loop off left hand needle,* K the st rem on left hand needle tog tbl with the next st on left hand needle again dropping only the 1st loop off needle, rep from * until 1 loop rem on left hand needle, K1 tbl.

2nd row P2 tog dropping only 1st loop off left hand needle, * P the st rem on left hand needle tog with next st on left hand needle again dropping only 1st loop off needle, rep from * until 1 loop rem on left hand needle, P1.

These 2 rows form the pattern and are repeated throughout.

Woven vertical rib

Worked over an even number of stitches, plus 2 edge stitches.

1st row K1, * yfwd, sl 1 knitwise K1, rep from * to last st, K1.

2nd row K1, * K1, K2 tog tbl thus working the slipped and the made stitch on previous row, rep from * to last st, K1.

These 2 rows form the pattern and are repeated throughout.

Fair Isle

These designs are all worked from the accompanying charts.

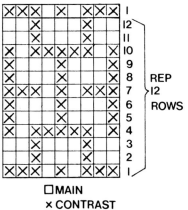

□ MAIN
× CONTRAST

Cast on a number of stitches divisible by 8 plus 1.

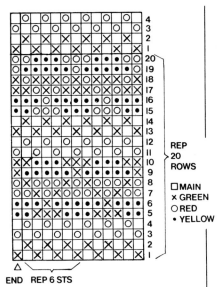

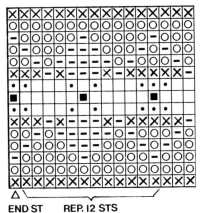

Cast on a number of stitches divisible by 6 plus 1.

REP 20 ROWS

□ MAIN
× GREEN
○ RED
• YELLOW

END REP 6 STS

END ST   REP. 12 STS

Cast on a number of stitches divisible by 12 plus 1.

Grafting

Two stocking stitch edges, knit side facing

Grafting is a method of joining two rows of stitches invisibly.

Have the stitches on two knitting needles, one behind the other, wrong sides of work together and needle points facing to the right. (Picture shows stitches slipped off needle with a contrast yarn being used for more clarity). As graft is to be invisible use the same yarn as garment.

Cut length of yarn, three to four times length of row to be grafted and thread into a blunt-ended needle. Insert needle into first stitch on front knitting needle as if to purl it and draw yarn through, leaving the stitch on the knitting needle. * Insert wool needle into first stitch on back knitting needle as if to purl it and slip it off knitting needle, then insert wool needle into next stitch on back needle as if to knit it and leave it on the knitting needle but draw yarn through. Insert wool needle into first stitch on front knitting needle as if to knit it and slip it off the knitting needle, then insert wool needle into next stitch on front needle as if to purl it leaving it on knitting needle but pulling yarn through. Now repeat from * until all the stitches have been worked off. Do not pull yarn too tight or leave it too slack, grafting stitches should be same size as knitted ones.

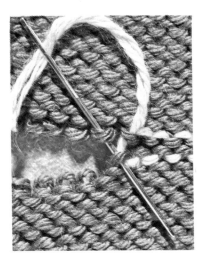

To join two edges of purl fabric
Work in same way as for stocking stitch, reading knit for purl and purl for knit. Or turn knitting to wrong side and work as for stocking stitch, turning to right side when grafting is finished.

Hems

Knitted in
Cast on required number of stitches and beginning with a knit row work an odd number of rows. Knit next row instead of purling it to mark fold line, now work one row less than number of rows that were worked initially, ending with a purl row. Before continuing with garment, pick up the stitches of the cast on row with an extra needle and hold these stitches behind stitches already on left hand needle. Knit to end of next

K

row by working one stitch from left hand needle together with one stitch from extra needle. Beginning with a purl row, continue in stocking stitch.

Picot

Cast on an odd number of stitches and beginning with a knit row work an even number of rows in stocking stitch. On the next row, or right side of work, make a row of picot eyelets by * K2 tog, yfwd, and repeat from * to last stitch, K1. Beginning with a purl row work the same number of rows as were worked initially to complete hem. When garment is finished, turn hem to wrong side of work at the picot row and slip stitch in place.

Reversed stocking stitch

When garment is completed,

leave stitches on needle instead of casting off and fold required depth of hem on to right side of work, so that the purl fabric forms the hem. Sew along the edge, taking one stitch from needle, one stitch from fabric. This method is ideal for finishing necklines or skirts which are worked from the waist down. It can also be made by folding hem to wrong side to form a plain stocking stitch edge.

Increasing

At the beginning of row

Knit required number of edge stitches (three in illustration), then knit in to the stitch below the next stitch on left hand needle, then increase by knitting into stitch immediately above.

At end of row

For left hand side of work, knit to one stitch before the edge stitches. Knit the next stitch, increase by knitting into stitch immediately below this stitch, then knit edge stitches.

Between stitches

If you are increasing knitwise (M1K) with right hand needle pick up yarn which lies between stitch just worked and next stitch and place it on left hand needle. Knit into back of this loop. This twists and tightens loop so that no hole is formed.
Slip loop off left hand needle, so making one stitch.
If you are increasing purlwise (M1P) work same way, but loop picked up is purled into from the back.

Invisible

Insert right hand needle into front of stitch below that on left hand needle and knit a new stitch. If increase is on purl work, then purl the new stitch. This method is particularly good when increase is not at end of a row, or does not form part of a pattern.

Party glitter in a simple and elegant evening top with narrow silver straps

K

To make a stitch between two knit stitches
Bring the yarn forward (yfwd) as if to purl, then back over the right hand needle ready to knit the next stitch.

To make a stitch between two purl stitches
Take the yarn over and round the needle (yrn).

To make a stitch between a knit and a purl stitch
Bring the yarn forward and once round the needle (yrn).

To make a stitch between a purl and a knit stitch
The yarn is already in position to the front and the next stitch is knitted in the usual way, the yarn taken over the needle (yon).

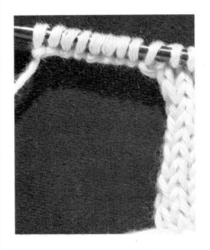

Multiple increasing
Cast on required number of stitches at the beginning of the side edge, using the two needle method. At end of row reverse the work and again cast on required number of stitches.

Jacquard

Jacquard knitting is the name given to patterned fabrics where more than one colour is used and where the pattern is knitted in at the same time as the background. This type of pattern can be shown on a chart. Where pattern consists of small repeats with only a few stitches in any one colour,

yarn not in use is carried loosely across back of work until needed again, then twisted round last colour used before beginning to knit with it again. If there are more than three stitches in any group, twist yarn not in use at regular intervals with yarn being used to avoid long strands of yarn across back of work. Where large blocks of colour are required it is best to use a separate ball of yarn for each area, twisting each new colour as it is brought into use with previous colour.

Hexagon pattern
When working this pattern, use a separate ball of yarn for each motif, and twist the yarns on the wrong side of work where they join on every row.
Using 3 colours, cast on 10 sts in each of the colours, A, B and C, making a number of stitches divisible by 30.
1st row *K10 C, K10 B, K10 A, rep from * to end.
2nd row *P10 A, P10 B, P10 C, rep from * to end.
3rd row As 1st.
4th row As 2nd.
5th row *K1 B, K8 C, K2 A, K8 B, K2 C, K8 A, K1 B, rep from * to end.
6th row *P2 B, P6 A, P4 C, P6 B, P4 A, P6 C, P2 B, rep from * to end.

Patchwork pull-on in a hexagon pattern finished with contrasting ribbing

K

7th row *K3 B, K4 C, K6 A, K4 B, K6 C, K4 A, K3 B, rep from * to end.

8th row *P4 B, P2 A, P8 C, P2 B, P8 A, P2 C, P4 B, rep from * to end.

9th row *K5 B, K10 A, K10 C, K5 B, rep from * to end.

10th row *P5 B, P10 C, P10 A, P5 B, rep from * to end.

11th to 12th rows Rep the 9th and 10th rows.

13th rows As 9th.

14th row As 8th.

15th row As 7th.

16th row As 6th.

17th row As 5th.

18th row As 2nd.

These 18 rows form the pattern.

Key pattern in three colours.
Using A cast on a number of stitches divisible by 8 plus 1.

1st row With A, K to end.

2nd row With A, P to end.

3rd row K2 A, *K1 B, K3 A, rep from * to last 3 sts, K1 B, K2 A.

4th row P1 A, *P1 B, P1 C, P1 B, P1 A, (P1 B, P1 A) twice rep from * to end.

5th row K1 B, *K3 A, K1 B, K3 C, K1 B, rep from * to end.

6th row P1 A, *P1 B, P1 C, P1 B, P5 A, rep from * to end.

7th row As 3rd.

8th row *P3 A, P1 B, P1 A, P1 B,

P1 C, P1 B, rep from * to last st, P1 A.

9th row K1 B, *K3 C, K1 B, K3 A, K1 B, rep from * to end.

10th row P1 A, *P1 B, P3 A, P1 B, P1 C, P1 B, P1 A, rep from * to end.

The 3rd to 10th rows form the pattern.

Note: If working this pattern as a border, rep the 3rd row at the end, to complete the pattern.

Wavy striped pattern
Using A cast on a number of stitches divisible by 4 plus 1.

1st row With A, K to end,

2nd row With A, P to end.

3rd row K1 B, *K3 A, K1 B, rep from * to end.

4th row P2 B, *P1 A, P3 B, rep

from * to last 3 sts, P1 A, P2 B.

5th row With B, K to end.

6th row With B, P to end.

7th row K1 C, *K3 B, K1 C, rep from * to end.

8th row P2 C, *P1 B, P3 C, rep from * to last 3 sts, P1 B, P2 C.

9th row With C, K to end.

10th row With C, P to end.

11th row K1 A, *K3 C, K1 A, rep from * to end.

12th row P2 A, *P1 C, P3 A, rep from * to last 3 sts, P1 C, P2 A.

These 12 rows form the pattern.

Loops

Picking up a loop four rows below
This is similar to knitting into a stitch on the previous row and is used in patterns with a stocking stitch background. Insert the right hand needle 4 or more rows below the stitch reached in the pattern and knit one, pulling up a long loop. Let the stitch drop from left hand needle until it reaches the row in which the loop stitch has been worked.

Picking up a loop with a crochet hook
Some novelty patterns require extra loops which are worked with the aid of a crochet hook. These loops are picked up knitwise several rows below. Knit to position where loop is required, leaving yarn at back of work.

Knitted like a sampler, a pull-on in random shapes, colours and stitches.

K

K

Insert crochet hook from front of work, 4 or more rows below and pull a long loop of yarn through to right side of work, making one extra long, loose stitch. Slip this extra stitch on to left hand needle and knit into the back of it together with next stitch on left hand needle. To transfer this loop diagonally across front of work leave it on crochet hook and work 3 or more stitches on to right hand needle in usual way. Then knit the extra loop together with next stitch on left hand needle.

Knitting a stitch with three loops
Begin with a knit row and wind yarn 3 times round right hand needle for each stitch. On next row, knit or purl these stitches as required, unwinding the 3 loops of each stitch and letting them drop off left hand needle.

Long wavy stitch
Worked over a number of stitches divisible by 7, plus 3 edge stitches.
1st row K to end.
2nd row K to end.
3rd row K3, * wind yarn twice round needle—called y2rn, (K1, y2rn) twice, K5, rep from * to end.
4th row K1, * K4, (drop yarn wound round needle and K next stitch) 3 times, this will lengthen the 3 sts which have been knitted, rep from * to last 2 sts, K2.
5th row K to end.
6th row K to end.
7th row K1, y2rn, *K5 (y2rn, K1) twice, y2rn, rep from * to last 2 sts, K2.
8th row K2, * (drop yarn round needle, K1) 3 times, K4, rep from * to last st, drop yarn round needle, K1.

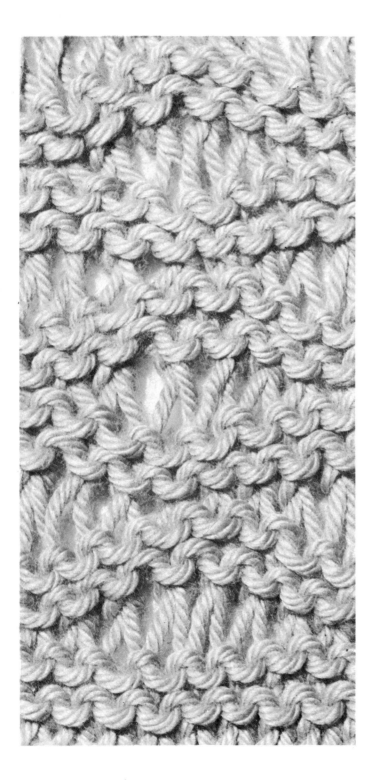

This pretty version of loopy knitting, called long wavy stitch, combines elongated loops with narrow bands of ordinary garter stitch.

The snowflake motif used for this afghan and matching cushion is a jacquard pattern based on a traditional Norwegian design. It uses only two colours on a contrasting background and is knitted in strips which are then joined, edged with crochet and finished with fringe.

K

Openwork stitches

Criss cross ladder

Worked over a number of stitches divisible by 8, plus 4.

1st row (wrong side) *P6, yrn, sl 1 purlwise, P1, psso, rep from * to last 4 sts, P4.

2nd row *K6, yfwd, sl 1 knitwise, K1, psso, rep from * to last 4 sts, K4.

These 2 rows form pattern and are repeated throughout.

Dimple

Cast on a number of stitches divisible by 3, plus 2.

1st row P to end.

2nd row P1, * yarn round right hand needle twice — called y2rn —, P1, rep from * to last st, P1.

3rd row P1, * slip next 3 sts p-wise on to right hand needle dropping extra loops (picture 1), pull the loose loops gently upwards and slip back on to left hand needle (picture 2), K3 tog tbl, bring yarn forward over right

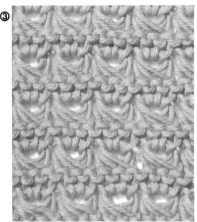

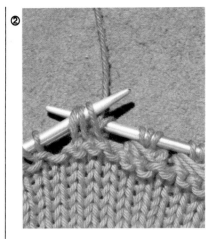

hand needle and back, then K3 tog tbl again, rep from * to last st, P1.

4th row P to end.

These 4 rows form pattern and are repeated throughout.

Faggotting cable stitch

Cast on a number of stitches divisible by 12 plus 8.

1st row (RS) P2, *K2, yfwd, sl 1, K1, psso, P2, rep from * to end.

2nd row K2, *P2, yrn, P2 tog, K2, rep from * to end.

Repeat these 2 rows twice more

7th row P2, K2, yfwd, sl 1, K1, psso, P2, *slip next 2 sts on to cable needle and hold at front of work, K2 from left hand needle then K2 from cable needle — called C4F —, P2, K2, yfwd, sl 1, K1, psso, P2, rep from * to end

8th row As 2nd.

Repeat the 1st and 2nd rows 3 times more.

15th row P2, C4F, P2, *K2, yfwd, sl 1, K1, psso, P2, C4F, P2, rep from * to end.

16th row As 2nd.

These 16 rows form the pattern.

Horseshoe stitch

Cast on a number of stitches divisible by 10 plus 1.

1st row (WS) P to end.

2nd row K1, *yfwd, K3, sl 1, K2 tog, psso, K3, yfwd, K1, rep from * to end.

3rd row P to end.

4th row P1, *K1, yfwd, K2, sl 1, K2, tog, psso, K2, yfwd, K1, P1,

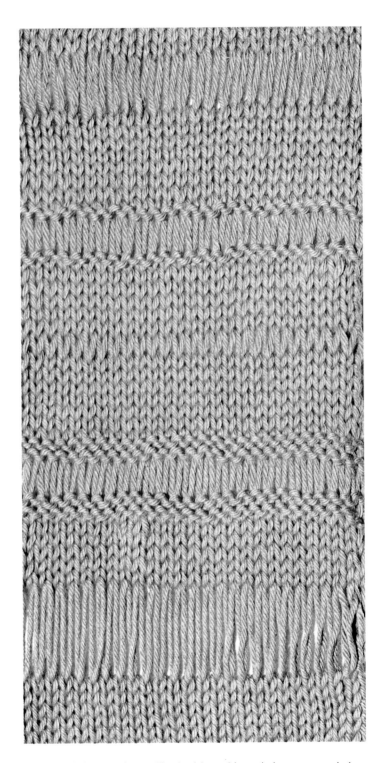

Loopy knitting can be combined with stocking stitch or garter stitch to form lacy openwork bands which are ideal for soft light stoles, scarves or evening blouses. The example shown here has looped bands of different widths, as in the technique described on page 126.

rep from * to end.

5th row K1, *P9, K1, rep from * to end.

6th row P1, *K2, yfwd, K1, sl 1, K2 tog, psso, K1, yfwd, K2, P1, rep from * to end.

7th row As 5th.

8th row P1, *K3, yfwd, sl 1, K2 tog, psso, yfwd, K3, P1, rep from * to end.

These 8 rows form the pattern.

Hortense

Cast on any number of stitches divisible by three.

1st and every alt row P to end.

2nd and every alt row *K1, bring the 2nd of the next 2 stitches across in front of the first, K2.

Repeat from * to end. These two rows form pattern.

Lace arrow pattern

Cast on a number of stitches divisible by 6 plus 1.

1st row K3, *yfwd, sl 1, K1, psso, K4, rep from * to last 4 sts, yfwd, sl 1, K1, psso, K2.

2nd and every alt row P to end

3rd row K1, *K2, tog, yfwd, K1, yfwd, sl 1, K1, psso, K1, rep from * to end.

5th row K2 tog, yfwd, *K3, yfwd, sl 1, K2 tog, psso, yfwd, rep from * to last 5 sts, K3, yfwd, sl 1, K1, psso.

7th row K1, *yfwd, sl 1, K1, psso, K1, K2, tog, yfwd, K1, rep from *

K

129

K

to end.
9th row As 7th.
10th row P to end.
These 10 rows form the pattern.

Openwork ladder
Worked over a number of stitches divisible by 10, plus 6.
1st row (wrong side) P6, *K2 tog tbl, wind yarn twice round needle, K2 tog, P6, rep from * to end.
2nd row K6, *P1, ·P into first made st and K into the second st, P1, K6, rep from * to end.
These 2 rows form the pattern and are repeated throughout.

Pimpernel
Worked over an odd number of stitches using two colours.

1st row With white, K.
2nd row With white, P.
3rd row With yellow, K1, *K2 tog, rep from * to end.
4th row With yellow, K1, * lift thread before next stitch and K into it, K1, rep from * to end.
These 4 rows form the pattern and are repeated throughout.

Ridged lace
Worked over a number of stitches divisible by 6, plus 1.
1st row *P1, P2 tog, yon, K1, yrn, P2 tog, rep from * to last st, P1.
2nd row P to end.
3rd row K to end.
4th row P to end.
These 4 rows form the pattern and are repeated throughout.

Seashell
Cast on a number of stitches divisible by 6, plus 2.
1st row K to end.
2nd row P to end.
Rep 1st and 2nd rows once more.

①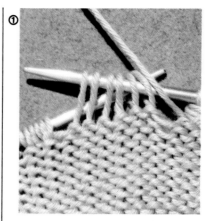

②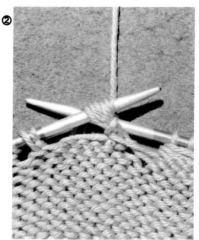

③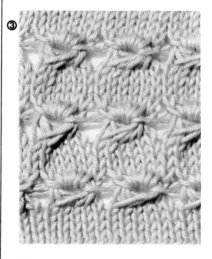

5th row K1, *y2rn, K1, rep from * to last st, K1.
6th row P1, * holding yarn at back of work slip next 6 sts p-wise on to right hand needle dropping extra loops (picture 1), pull the loose stitches gently upwards and slip back on to left hand needle (picture 2), yrn and P6 tog with-

K

out slipping them off left hand needle, yon and K1 into these 6 sts, then P1, K1 into same 6 sts in usual way, rep from * to last st, P1.

These 6 rows form pattern and are repeated throughout.

Spider lace stitch

Cast on a number of stitches divisible by 6 plus 1.

1st row K1, *K2 tog, yfwd, K1, yfwd, sl 1, K1, psso, K1, rep from * to end.

2nd and every alt row P to end

3rd row K2 tog, *yfwd, K3, yfwd, sl 1, K2 tog, psso, rep from * to last 5 sts, yfwd, K3, yfwd, sl 1, K1, psso.

5th row K1, *yfwd, sl 1, K1, psso, K1, K2 tog, yfwd, K1, rep from * to end.

7th row As 5th.

9th row As 5th.

11th row K2, *yfwd, sl 1, K2 tog, psso, yfwd, K3, rep from * to last 5 sts, yfwd, sl 1, K2 tog, psso, yfwd, K2.

12th row As 2nd.

These 12 rows form the pattern.

Trefoil rib pattern

Cast on a number of stitches divisible by 6 plus 1.

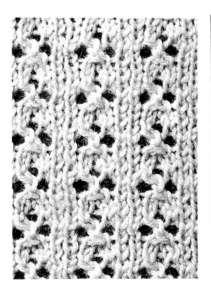

1st row P1, *K5, P1, rep from * to end.

2nd row K1, *P5, K1, rep from * to end.

3rd row P1, *K1, yfwd, sl 1, K2 tog, psso, yfwd, K1, P1, rep from * to end.

4th row As 2nd.

5th row P1, *K2, yfwd, sl 1, K1, psso, K1, P1, rep from * to end

6th row As 2nd.

These 6 rows form the pattern.

Wavy

Worked over an even number of stitches.

1st row K1, *yrn, P2 tog, rep from * to last st, K1.

2nd row P.

These 2 rows form the pattern and are repeated throughout.

Picking up stitches

Using either needle or crochet hook

This method of finishing a neckline or other edge saves the trouble of casting on a separate collar, cuff or edging and seaming it on when completing the garment. Pick up stitches with right side of work facing you. You can use the knitting needle which is going to be used to knit the edging. Hold yarn behind work and insert tip of needle through the stitch, drawing through a loop of yarn to right side and forming one loop on needle. Continue until all required stitches are on needle. A crochet hook can be used to draw yarn loop through as illustrated, loop is then slipped on to needle to be used.

Pockets

Flap

When working an inserted pocket, make the inside flap first. Calculate number of stitches needed for pocket and cast on this number plus an extra two stitches. Work in stocking stitch for required length of pocket and cast off.

Work outside pocket flap in size and pattern desired and leave these stitches on a holder. Now work in stocking stitch on front of garment until position for pocket is reached, ending with a right side row. On next row purl until

K

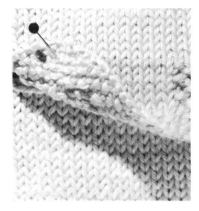

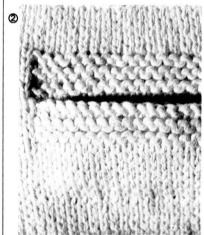

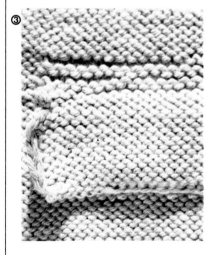

pocket opening stitches are reached, cast off pocket opening stitches knitwise and purl to end of row. Place needle holding outside pocket flap stitches in front of the main fabric with the right side facing you, knit to the cast off opening stitches then knit across the pocket flap stitches in place of those cast off and knit to end of remaining stitches. Place inside pocket flap behind stitch opening on wrong side and stitch neatly in place (2).

Inserted pocket with garter stitch edge

Make inside flap first and leave these stitches on a holder until required. Calculate number of stitches needed for pocket and cast on this number plus an extra two stitches. Work in stocking stitch for required length of pocket, knitting two stitches together at each end of last row and leave

stitches for time being. Now work front of garment in stocking stitch until position for pocket is reached, less four rows, ending with a right side row and making sure that you allow for depth of inside pocket flap. With wrong side of

work facing, purl until pocket opening stitches are reached, knit across these stitches, then purl to end of row. Work a further three rows, working in garter stitch across pocket opening stitches, then cast off pocket opening stitches knitwise. Place needle holding inside flap stitches behind the main fabric with right side facing, knit to cast off opening stitches then knit across inside flap stitches in place of those cast off and knit to end of row (1). Continue in stocking stitch, working three more rows in garter stitch across pocket opening stitches (2). When work is completed, stitch down inside flap neatly to wrong side of work (3).

Pompon

For large pompons, a cardboard frame is required. Decide on diameter of pompon and draw two circles of this diameter on to cardboard. From centre of each circle cut out a smaller circle: the larger this inner circle, the more wool needed to complete pompon and heavier it will be when finished (1).

Place the two circles together and with one or more strands of yarn begin to wind around frame as evenly as possible (2).

When centre hole is almost filled, thread yarn into a blunt pointed needle and continue until hole is completely filled.

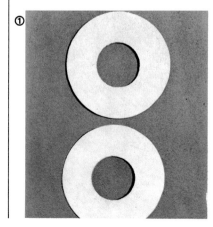

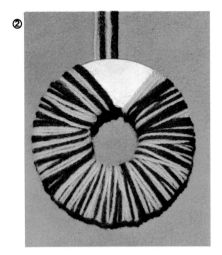

②

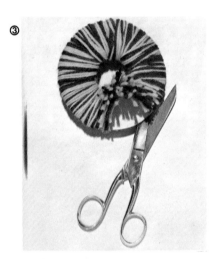

③

④

Take a sharp pair of scissors and begin to cut strands of yarn at outside edge, working in line with edge of cardboard, placing scissors between cardboard circles (3). Gently, with tips of scissors, begin

Pretty pompons: add them to cushions, a nursery rug or cot cover. Use one to make a 'pull' for a roller blind or trim a woolly cap.

K

to open cardboard rings until they are far enough apart for you to tie a strong strand of yarn tightly round all the threads where they pass through centre of rings. If pompon is to be sewn on to a garment, leave ends of yarn hanging so they can be used for sewing on. Once centre is tied, continue to remove both rings of cardboard. Fluff pompon into a complete ball and trim uneven ends.

Seaming

Back stitch

This is worked in a similar way to that used in dressmaking. Whether you work half or a whole stitch in from the edge may be determined by the thickness of garment being seamed. Start by working two small stitches, one on top of the other. * Now, with needle at back of work, move along to left, bringing needle through to front of work the width of one stitch away from last stitch. Take needle back to left hand end of last stitch and take it through to back of work. Repeat from * until seam is complete. Pull stitches firmly through knitting but be careful not to draw it too tight, nor stretch the seam.

Chain stitch

This makes a flat seam that is useful for sewing in sleeves. Pin pieces together, right sides facing and sew seam with chain stitch as

shown in picture. To stitch knitting, use a blunt pointed needle as it is less likely to split the stitches. If garment has been made in a fairly thick yarn, either split the yarn for seaming or buy a thinner one in the same shade.

Invisible

Begin by securing sewing yarn to one side. Pass needle directly across to other side of work, picking up one stitch. Pass needle directly back to first side of work, picking up one loop. Continue working in this way as if making rungs on a ladder, but pull stitches tight so that they are not visible on right side when finished. All seams should be pressed on wrong side with damp cloth after completion.

Slipped stitches

Knitwise on a knit row

Hold yarn behind work as if to knit stitch. Insert right hand

needle point into stitch from front to back, as if to knit and slip it on to right hand needle. When a slip stitch forms part of a decrease on a knit row, stitch must be slipped knitwise. In working a pattern, however, where the slip stitch is not part of a decrease, it must be slipped purlwise on a knit row to prevent it becoming crossed when purled in following row.

Purlwise on a purl row

Hold yarn at front of work as if to purl stitch. Insert right hand needle point from back to front as if to purl, and slip it on to right hand needle. On a purl row make sure you slip the stitch purlwise.

Tassel

Cut a piece of card, its width being

required length of tassel. Wind yarn round and round card until desired thickness is obtained. Using a blunt ended needle threaded with yarn, insert needle at one edge of card, under the strands, taking them all together and fasten off securely. Cut through strands of yarn at other untied edge of card. Finish tassel by winding an end of yarn several times round the top, slightly below tied end, fasten off securely, leaving an end long enough to secure tassel to garment.

Tubular knitting

Moss stitch
Work as for ribbed method below, but take care always to knit the purl stitch and purl the knit stitch of previous rows.

Ribbed
Cast on double the number of

stitches required, having a multiple of 4.

1st row (K1, P1) across half the stitches, turn and fold work in half.

2nd row Using a third needle for this row only, *K1 from the front needle, yfwd, sl 1 P-wise from back needle, P1 from front needle, sl 1 P-wise from back needle, rep from * to end.

3rd row *K1, yfwd, sl 1 P-wise, P1, sl 1 P-wise, ybk, rep from * to end.

Repeat the 3rd row for the length required.

Stocking stitch
Cast on double the number of stitches, having an even number.

1st row To work in reverse stocking stitch (1), P across half the stitches, turn and fold work in

half.

2nd row Using a 3rd needle, *P1 from front needle, sl 1 P-wise from back needle, repeat from * to end.

3rd row *P1, sl 1 P-wise, rep from * to end.

Repeat the 3rd row for length required. To work in ordinary stocking stitch (2); K across half the stitches, turn and fold work in half.

2nd row Using a third needle, *K1 from front needle, yfwd, sl 1 P-wise from back needle, ybk, rep from * to end.

3rd row *K1, yfwd, sl 1 P-wise, ybk, rep from * to end.

Repeat the 3rd row for the length required.

To cast off
It is necessary to open up the tube: slip the stitches off the needle and replace them on two

135

K

needles, putting the front stitches on to one needle and the back stitches on to a second needle, then cast off in the normal way.

V-neckline

Single rib neckband with centre shaping combining two methods of decreasing

Cast on required number of stitches noting that centre stitch must be a knit stitch for right side of work. Mark centre stitch with coloured thread.

1st row (right side) Work in K1, P1 rib to within 1 st of centre st ending with P1, sl the next st K-wise, K centre st and next st tog, psso, beg with P1 rib to end.
2nd row Rib to 1 st before centre st, P next 3 sts tog, beg with P1 rib to end.
Rep these 2 rows for required depth of neckband. Cast off in rib still decreasing at centre point, or cast off invisibly.

Single rib neckband with centre stitch combining two methods of decreasing

Cast on required number of stitches noting that centre stitch must be a knit stitch for right side of work. Mark centre stitch with coloured thread.

1st row (right side) Work in K1, P1 rib to within 2 sts of centre st ending with P1, sl 1, K1, psso,

K centre st, K2 tog, beg with P1 rib to end.
2nd row Rib to 2 sts before centre st, sl 1, K1, psso, P centre st, K2 tog, beg with P1 rib to end.
Rep these 2 rows for required depth of neckband. Cast off in rib still decreasing at centre point, or cast off invisibly.

Single rib neckband with centre stitch, using slip stitch decreasing

Cast on the required number of stitches noting that the centre stitch must be a knit stitch for the right side of the work Mark the centre stitch with coloured thread.

1st row (right side) Work in K1, P1 rib to within 2 sts of centre st ending with P1, K next 2 sts tog tbl, K centre st, K next 2 sts tog, beg with P1 rib to end.
2nd row Rib to 2 sts before centre st, P2 tog, P centre st, P2 tog, beg with P1 rib to end.

Rep these 2 rows for required depth of neckband Cast off in rib still decreasing at centre point, or cast off invisibly.

Single rib neckband with centre shaping using slip stitch decreasing

Cast on required number of stitches noting that centre stitch must be a purl stitch for right side of work. Mark centre stitch with coloured thread.

1st row (right side) Work in K1, P1 rib to within 1 st of centre st ending with K1, sl next st and centre st P-wise, P next st and pass 2 slipped sts over this st, beg with K1, work in rib to end.
2nd row Rib to 1 st before centre st, sl next st and centre st K-wise, P next st and pass 2 slipped sts over this st, beg with K1 rib to end.
Rep these 2 rows for required depth of neckband. Cast off in rib, still decreasing at centre point, or cast off invisibly. All above neckbands are worked on two needles, allowing for a seam at centre back of neck. They can also be added to a garment by picking up stitches round neck, but one shoulder should be left unseamed so neckband can be worked in rows. Count number of rows on right and left fronts from centre 'V' point and allow one stitch for every row and one stitch for every stitch of the back neck cast off stitches.

L

Lace

Venetian and Burano

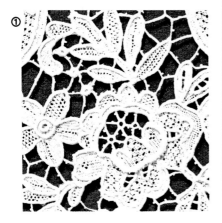

Venetian lace, as well as the lace from the neighbouring island of Burano, are the most precious and sought after of Italian laces. Both are similarly worked but are differentiated by their backgrounds. Venetian lace (1) has an openwork background, the motifs being linked by bars, with or without picots. Burano lace (2) has a tulle background. The design for the lace is drawn in ink on to a special type of paper, this is tacked on to several layers of firm fabric as a support for the lace. Motifs are worked like Renaissance lace and then the appropriate background, finally motifs are outlined with buttonhole stitch, the lace is removed from the paper and carefully ironed.

Ladder, overcast

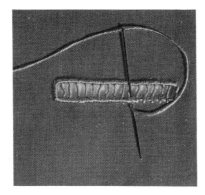

First work a row of small running stitches to delineate the outline, then with sharp scissors cut a small hole in the left hand corner. Work close overcasting as far as position of first bar. Take thread across to other side, then overcast back again to cover bar. Continue in the same way to length of ladder required, then overcast ends and upper edge.

Long and short stitch

This should be worked in a frame. It is worked rather like satin stitch and takes its name from the irregular method of starting the first row of stitches. Start at the outline and make the first row of stitches alternately long and short,

following outline closely. Then fill in rest of shape with rows of stitches of the same length, fitting them into the spaces left by the row before to give a smooth texture. Length of stitch should only vary when filling in uneven shapes when stitches should be carefully graded to produce a neat finish.

Loops

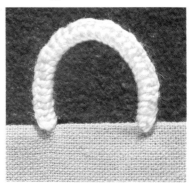

For buttons

Measure width of loop needed, this should be a little less than radius of button, mark this distance with 2 pins placed at right angles to edge of garment. Join thread at point marked by first pin. Pick up a small piece of fabric at second pin. Repeat three times. Work buttonhole stitch over these threads, keeping stitches close together.

For hooks and belts

Worked similarly to button loops,

137

L

but across fabric instead of on the edge. Take care not to pick up threads of fabric when working the buttonhole stitch. Thread used depends on purpose of loop.

Hanging loop sewn to corner

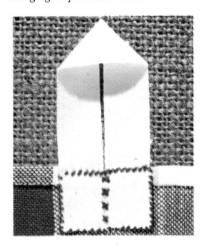

Hanging loop sewn to straight edge

Tape

Useful for hanging tea towels or dishcloths. Take a piece of tape about 16cm (6in) long. Fold in half, making top of fold into triangular shape. If loop is to be sewn to corner, pin in position on wrong side. Attach with over-sewing, round corner and edges of tape, finishing centre with cross stitches as shown in first picture. If loop is to be sewn to one side, attach as shown in second picture. (Use matching thread).

Wall hanging embroidered in long and short and chain stitch. A roughly textured linen is an ideal contrast to the smooth embroidery.

Macrame

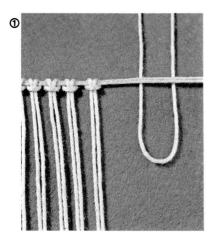

Setting on doubled knotting thread

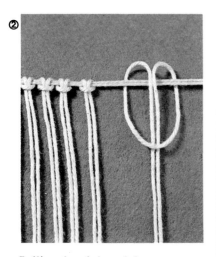

Pulling thread through loop

Setting on threads

You can use any thread for macramé, as long as it is twisted, strong and smooth. Stretch the horizontal foundation threads tautly and secure with pins and set on the doubled knotting threads as shown. When doing a large piece of work you will find it easier to wind surplus thread into small bundles secured with an elastic band from which you can feed it out as required. To work directly on to fabric, pull the double threads through the fabric with a crochet hook and loop them as shown in (2). Each double thread must be 4 times length of finished article.

Basic cording knot

Begin the macramé with a row of cording to give it a firm base. Attach a second foundation thread at top left hand side of work, immediately below the setting on knots. Hold this thread taut in a horizontal position with right hand. Working from left to right, bring each knotting thread up in turn and wrap it round the foundation thread twice to form a knot. Pull each cording knot tightly into place before going on to the next.

Cavandoli

This technique uses only two colours and the basic cording knot, both horizontally and vertically. The horizontal knotting provides the background and the vertical knots form the pattern.

The vertical cording knot is the same as the horizontal but the hanging thread is used as leader and a second thread is knotted down the length of this leader. The knotting thread always starts by passing behind the leader so that when travelling across the work to the right the knots face to the right and when returning across work on next row, knots point to the left.

The threads in the background colour are set on the foundation thread and the ball of thread in the pattern colour is attached to the left hand corner of the work, from where it is used as a leader

for the horizontal cording or used to make the vertical cording knots which form the pattern. Designs can be worked out on squared paper using crosses for pattern and blank squares for background, but remember that Cavandoli elongates the pattern. It is traditional to work the first and last threads in vertical cording with a little picot when thread is turned to form a pretty border.

Allow for at least eight times length of finished article for background colour threads. The pattern colour is all in one ball and equals the length of all the background threads added together. Should thread run out, sew in the ends and attach new lengths very neatly.

To begin, attach pattern to knotting board. Pin the ends of the holding cord alongside and set on

M

the correct number of doubled threads in background colour.

Attach pattern thread to top left hand side of holding thread. Secure it by making one vertical cording knot on the first thread and then, using the pattern thread as leader, work a row of horizontal cording. At end of row work a vertical cording knot on the last thread with the pattern thread, then loop it round a pin to form a picot, return to the end thread and pass the pattern thread under the background thread to work another vertical knot. In this way, knotting is worked in opposite direction to previous row. Continue with horizontal cording and vertical cording at each end, inserting vertical cording knots where they are shown on pattern.

When finishing work, ends can

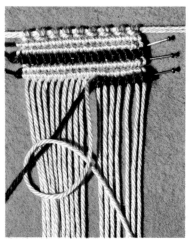

either be fringed, sewn in or knotted. For fringing, work two rows of horizontal cording first to secure ends.

To decrease width of a braid, such as a strap or belt, reduce one stitch on every row after required length has been reached. Make first vertical knot on every row over two threads instead of one then pin out outside thread to one side until article is finished, when ends are sewn in.

Thread used should be strong and smooth enough for easy running. Crochet and knitting cottons, macramé twine and fine string are all suitable. Some double knitting wools are strong enough for chair covers and bags, while rug wool and heavier strings can be used for mats and floor coverings. As patterns are tightly knotted it is unwise to choose too stiff a thread or one which will snap under the tension.

Cavandoli watchstraps are decorative and very quickly made accessories.

M

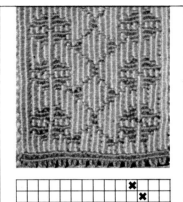

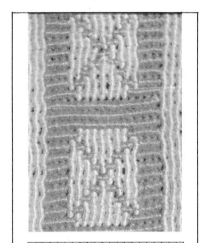

Decorative headings

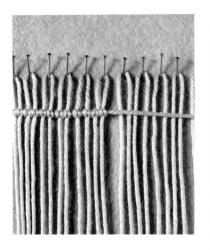

Picots (simple)

Pin doubled threads behind the foundation cord. Attach to the cord with cording.

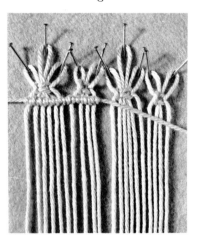

Picots (knotted)

Place three doubled threads side by side behind the foundation cord with the centre thread slightly higher than those on either side. Work a flat knot using the four central threads as a core. Fix with cording to foundation cord. Alternate picots are made with two smaller loops, using two centre threads as a core for the flat knot.

Scallops

Pin doubled threads as for simple picots, but using three, one inside

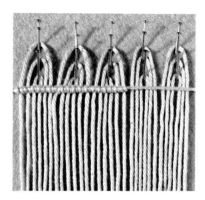

the other. Keep spacing even by careful pinning. Cord to the foundation.

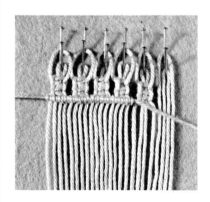

Scallops (knotted)

Pin two doubled threads, one inside the other. Work two flat knots and then attach the scallops to the foundation cord with cording.

Scallops (double knotted)

Pin two doubled threads as for knotted scallops. Work a pair of double knotted chains. Attach to a second foundation cord with cording (doubled threads are pinned over first foundation cord).

One of the joys of macramé is that the basic patterns adapt very easily to practically any article you wish to make. The bag shown here is made up in a Persian pattern with a simple picot heading and fringe, the long plaited handle is finished with tasselled ends.

M

Diagonal cording

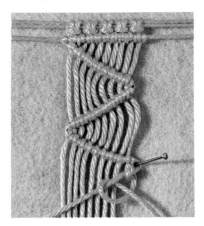

The basic cording knot can be worked diagonally, sloping to the right or left. This is used to form a braid or diamond patterned fabric. For a decorative braid about 2.5cm (1in) wide use a no.3 crochet cotton and set on 6 double knotting threads.

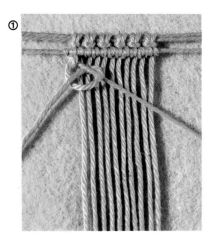

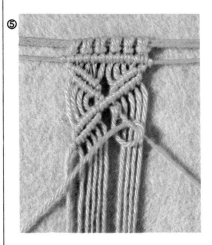

Diamond pattern in diagonal cording
The left hand pair of knotting threads are used as knot carriers when working from left to right and the right hand pair when working from right to left. These threads are called leaders and should be at least 4 times length of finished work. Finish off ends by making a row of horizontal cording and either darn ends back in or make a fringe.

(1) Hold first leader thread at an angle of 45 degrees and knot the second leader over it. Continue working first row of cording knots to the centre of the set-on threads.
(2) Make another row of cording parallel to the first, working with the second leader as the knot carrier.
(3) Repeat from the right, always using the leaders as knot carriers.
(4) Make a cording knot with second leaders in the centre.
(5) Repeat movements working out from centre left, then right. Return to step (1) and continue for required length.

Flat knots

This knot is another of the basic movements of macramé. Worked in series it makes intricate braids

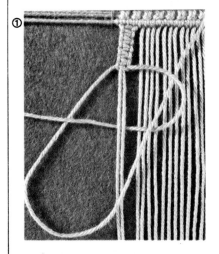

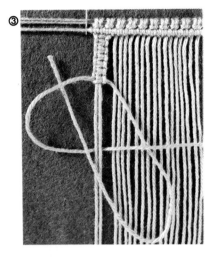

which can take on entirely different looks depending on the yarn used.

(1) Set on threads in multiples of four and work a line of cording. The centre two threads of each group of four act as a core over which the right and left hand threads are knotted. Hold the two centre threads taut in your left hand by winding them round the third finger. With right hand, form right hand thread into a loop with the end passing under the centre core and over the left hand thread. Then bring left hand thread over the core and thread it through the loop from the front of work.

(2) Pull both threads up until the knot closes tightly round the centre core. This completes the first part of the knot.

(3) Repeat the process in reverse order, forming the left hand thread into a loop, passing the right hand thread through as illustrated.

(4) Tighten threads to complete knot.

This piece of macramé combines diagonal cording, double knotted chains and flat knots with bobbles; it would make a pretty lampshade.

M

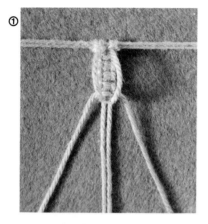

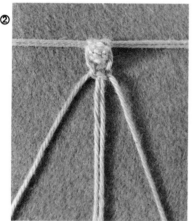

Flat knots with bobbles

Work two flat knots, then using a tapestry needle, thread the two central threads from front to back through the work above the centre of the first knot (1). Pull up until a little blackberry shaped roll is formed. The next knot you work will hold the ball in place. (2) For a larger bobble work either four or six flat knots.

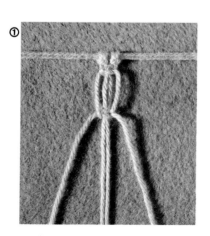

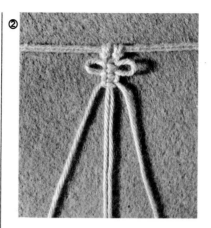

Flat knots with picots

Work one flat knot and then a second leaving a space between them (1). Push the knot up into place under the first one.(2). The length of thread left between the two knots dictates the size of the picot.

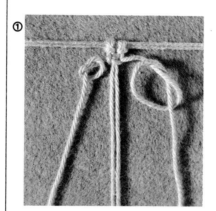

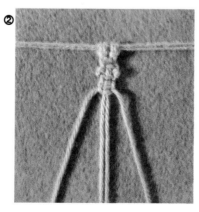

Flat knots with side knots

Work one flat knot then tie a simple knot on each of the right and left hand threads as shown in step (1). Use a pin to slide the knots up against the preceding flat knot before finally tightening it. Make a second flat knot. (2).

Knotted chains

Knotting single thread to right
Working with a doubled thread, hold the left thread firmly with the left hand. With right hand, knot right thread as shown.

Knotting single thread to left
Work in same way as above, but holding right thread firm and knotting left one as shown. Chains are made by alternating knots from left to right.

Macramé sash and matching headband decorated with fringing and exotic glass beads

146

M

With double loops

Working with a doubled thread, hold the left thread firmly with thumb and forefinger of left hand. Then, using right hand, knot the other thread alternately to the right and left.

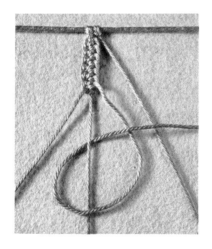

With three threads

Start with two doubled threads, but continue with only three, moving the fourth to one side as shown. Hold the central thread firmly with the second and third fingers of the left hand and with the outside threads make a knotted chain, once to the left, once to the right. This shows how knotted chains can be varied depending on the effect that is required.

Double knotted chain

Made in the same way as a single knotted chain, alternating knots

from left to right and using doubled threads if a thicker chain is required.

Maltese tufts embroidery

These are best worked in simple geometric groupings and make an ideal decoration for soft furnishings such as cushions. Felt or firmly woven cotton or linen make good backgrounds for this technique. Use either a smooth soft wool or thick soft cotton yarn. Position each tuft by counting threads on the background fabric and marking a 6mm ($\frac{1}{4}$in) wide line where tuft is required. Size of each tuft depends on scale of overall design, but 6mm ($\frac{1}{4}$in) wide is about the ideal for tufts worked

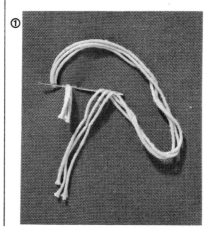

on an average linen weave. Use a large tapestry needle (no. 18 or 20) and three or four strands of yarn. Working from right to left, insert needle from front of fabric at a point a quarter of the way along from the right on the marked line. Bring needle out at left hand end of line and pull through, leaving loose end to form half the tuft. Next take a back stitch, inserting needle at right hand end of the line and bringing it out three quarters of the way along (1). Pull yarn through firmly and trim ends evenly to required length (2).

Mending
Darning knitting

Over vertical threads

If fabric has actually worn right through and formed a hole, threads must be placed over the gap before the stitches can be worked. Thread a blunt ended wool needle with matching yarn and pass it through centre of a stitch at lower right hand side of the hole, leaving end on wrong side to be darned in. Insert needle from right to left round both threads of stitch at top of hole immediately above. Draw thread through and pass it through lower stitch once again from front to back. Repeat, joining each

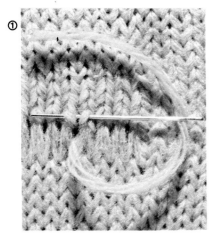

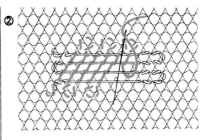

lower stitch to the one immediately above until all stitches are stranded together. Care should be taken to keep thread tension even so that the hole is not drawn smaller. Thread the wool needle again and draw the yarn through between two strands in the centre of the stitch at top right hand corner, drawing yarn through from back to front and leaving an end for darning in on wrong side. Insert needle from right to left round the two strands of stitch immediately above and draw yarn through as shown in step (1). Return yarn through to wrong side next to first stitch brought through to right side as shown in step (2). Continue along first row in this way until row is complete. Using this row, work one row lower down the vertical strands. Continue to fill hole, matching rows of stitches with knitting fabric so that tension for finished darn appears the same.

Over horizontal threads

Count number of downward stitches that need replacing and work a corresponding number of horizontal strands, using exactly matching yarn (contrast is only used in illustrations for clarity). Now, working upwards, insert needle from right to left and make 'half' stitches as shown. Work next row of half stitches downwards to complete the V effect.

Darning net

Holes in net are darned by duplicating the formation of the net itself, using closely matching thread. This method produces an almost invisible repair.
(1) Begin by working the horizontal threads, making sure that stitches are worked beyond the width of the damaged part by at least two holes at each end.
(2) Work from left to right, beginning two holes below the bottom row of horizontal threads. Loop thread once round each of the horizontal threads working diagonally upwards.

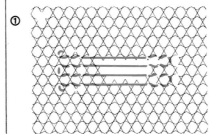

(3) Again work from left to right, beginning two holes above top row of horizontal threads and working diagonally downwards. Finish thread off firmly.

Darning, reinforcing

These darns are worked to strengthen threads which already exist but have worn thin. Darn across weft threads only unless area has worn so thin that this would not give adequate support. Stitching is worked on wrong side of fabric. Small running stitches are worked back and forth across thin area, keeping rows of stitches as close as possible. On woollen fabric, leave small loops at ends of each row to allow for shrinkage, the finished darn remains flat on the right side.

M

'Invisible' repair

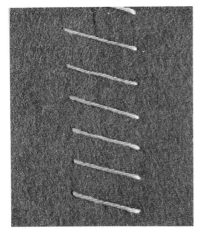

Clean tear, drawn together with large contrasting oversewing stitches

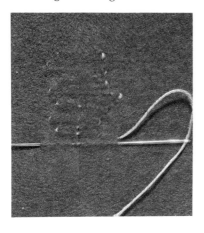

Use matching thread for final stitching (contrast used for clarity here).

This is generally used for a clean cut or tear on a thick woollen fabric. However, if surrounding threads are damaged, do not cut these away as they can be worked over in the repair. To draw torn edges together as closely as possible, first tack fabric to a piece of paper, then work large oversewing stitches using contrasting thread which will be removed when repair is completed. Now, working upwards, stitch the tear with tiny running stitches, starting and ending about 1cm ($\frac{3}{8}$in) each side of tear. Take stitches through the thickness of the fabric, drawing edges of tear together but not overlapping.

Patching

A patch should be as inconspicuous as possible and to achieve this the material and thread used for sewing must be closely matched to the article to be mended.

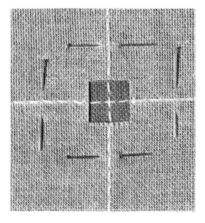

Woven

First neaten edges of hole into a square or rectangular shape. Then, using a piece of identical fabric, cut a patch measuring 5 or 6cm (2 to 2$\frac{1}{2}$in) larger than the hole all round. Mark centres of patch and hole. Place patch on wrong side, matching centres and pin it. Carefully draw out one thread on all four sides of patch so that drawn thread lies one thread beyond edge of hole. Starting on left, cut along left hand drawn thread until horizontal intersection is reached. Fold patch upwards from intersection and pin back. Now unravel first thread from cut edge of patch, thread it

into a needle and darn back into torn fabric. Continue along the side of hole (the threads secure the patch to the fabric around outer edges of hole). When first side is completed, turn work, cut along the next line marked by the drawn thread, pin patch back and continue as before. Finish all four sides in this manner.

Plain

Because they are strong, flat and easy to launder, hemmed patches are used for articles which require frequent washing such as shirts or household linen. Cut a piece of fabric large enough to cover the hole and the surrounding area, plus 0.5cm ($\frac{1}{4}$in) turnings. Tack turnings to right side of patch and mitre corners so that they are neat and square. Place patch in posi-

①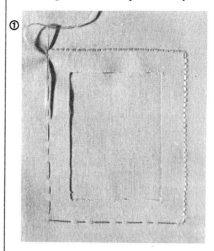

②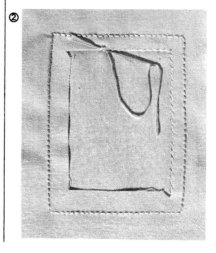

150

tion, matching weft and warp threads with right side of patch facing wrong side of garment. Pin and then tack patch in place. Working on right side and using a matching thread, back stitch or machine stitch article to patch (1). Always begin stitching in the middle of a side to avoid weakness at corners. Remove tacking and press. Still working on right side, trim hole to a square shape and then snip diagonally into each corner. Turn under the raw edges and hem fabric to patch.

Patterned

Cut a square patch from matching fabric (1) as for plain patch taking care that patterns match exactly. Tack turnings to wrong side of patch and mitre corners. With wrong side of patch to

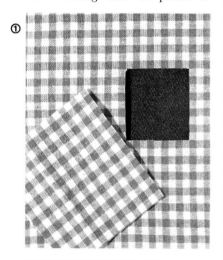

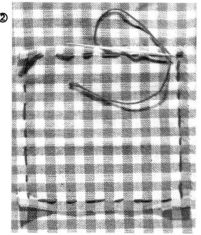

right side of garment, pin and tack in place. Hem patch (2) taking small stitches very close together. Turn to inside of work. Trim hole to square shape and snip diagonally into corners. Press back raw edges and oversew to neaten (3).

Reinforcing knitting

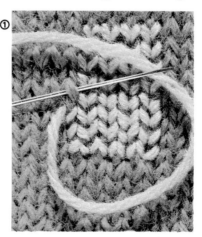

Method 1

If area to be strengthened is wearing thin but is not actually a hole, the outline of the existing stitches should be followed. Thread a blunt-ended wool needle with exactly matching yarn and working upwards insert the needle from right to left under one thread of the stitch immediately above and to the right (1). Draw yarn through and continue working up all the stitches to be strengthened. This has completed half a row of stitches. To work the other half,

pass the needle behind the last stitch and bring it out two threads to the left, work down the next row of stitches to complete the V effect.

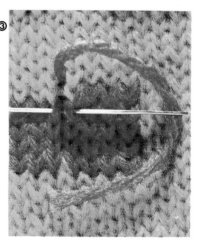

Method 2

Insert needle from right to left under both threads of the stitch immediately above the one that is to be covered (2) and draw yarn through. Insert needle back into base of stitch where yarn first passed through to the right side of front of the work and draw yarn through. Do not pull yarn tightly when drawing it through or the original fabric will pucker and the new stitch will not cover the old one properly. Continue in this way until all the stitches that need strengthening have been covered completely (3).

M

Re-weaving darns

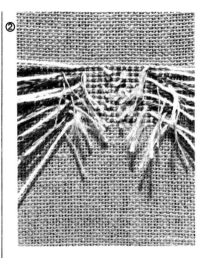

Small hole

Darns involving the re-weaving of fabric to fill a hole are usually worked on woven fabrics. Study the weave of the fabric through a magnifying glass before starting to darn, so that you can duplicate it with your stitches. Threads for re-weaving darns are drawn from an unseen part of the garment. Quite short lengths of thread can be used as, on each row of darning the ends of threads are left free and a new thread used to begin next row. Place work in an embroidery frame to hold fabric taut, wrong side up. Working from area outside hole, stitch the darning thread through the fabric, working over and under existing threads and then across the hole (top). After completing darning one way, turn work and darn the other way. Make sure that needle is passed through darning threads in exactly the same way as fabric is woven. After hole has been filled, clip ends of threads about 3mm ($\frac{1}{8}$in) from surface of fabric. Press the mend.

Small hole (patterned)

This is worked on the same principle as re-weaving a small hole in plain fabric but remember that you will need to match both warp and weft threads of each colour in the patterns as the illustrations show.

Tears

A clean cut or a hedge tear without a surrounding worn area can

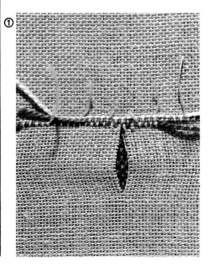

be mended almost invisibly with a woven darn. Close edges of tear with fishbone stitch. Using threads drawn from inside of garment, darn across slit, working on wrong side, using the re-weaving method and working over an area of about 1.5cm ($\frac{1}{2}$in) on each side.

Seaming

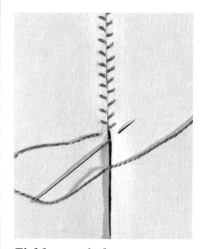

Fishbone stitch

This is used for drawing the edges of tears together before they are repaired, but fishbone stitch can be used without further darning if the slit is very small. Working on wrong side of fabric, fasten the thread with a few running stitches at one end of tear and then pass needle, from the back, through on one side of the slit about 3mm ($\frac{1}{8}$in) from it. Take needle through slit and bring it through from the back on the other side of slit.

Take it back through slit again this time passing it over previous stitch which lies in the centre of slit, thus pulling stitch down.

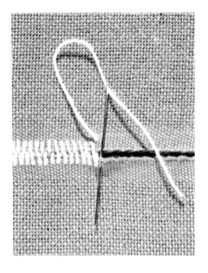

Fishbone (horizontal)

The fishbone stitching is worked more closely and is used to conceal a join between two selvedges. Pass needle first under two threads of the upper selvedge and then under two threads of lower selvedge. Space each stitch about two threads apart.

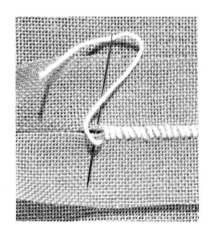

Folded edges

On wrong side fold each piece of fabric to be joined about 1cm ($\frac{3}{8}$in) from edge. Bring folded edges together and oversew, picking up two threads from one side and two threads from the other. (Seam is shown opened out for clarity).

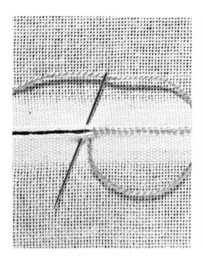

Oversewing

Also used for joining selvedges. Work from right to left or vice versa. Do not pull thread too tightly when oversewing as this will cause two edges to overlap.

Mitred corner

Folded mitre

Tack along lines where hem must be folded at corner. Crease across the corner diagonally, then fold the corner in two at right angles to the crease. Sew the two thicknesses together along crease. Trim turnings close to stitching. Turn corner right side out and press, making quite sure that stitched line bisects corner exactly. Finish hem in normal way.

Mitred facing

Cut facing strips and seam together diagonally as shown above. Trim turnings close to seam and press. With right sides together, apply facing to garment. Tack

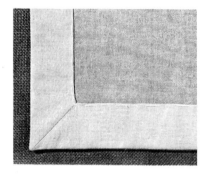

and sew round outside edges. Turn to inside, tack and hem inner edge of facing in place.

Monograms

Embroidered initials, whether simply or elaborately worked add a distinctive touch to clothes or household linen. This example is worked in satin stitch and cording. Transfer required letters on to fabric and pad the solid areas with rows of running stitch, back stitch or chain stitch. The fine lines are padded with back stitch or stem stitch. Solid areas are then worked over in satin stitch and the fine lines in cording.

N

Needle-made lace

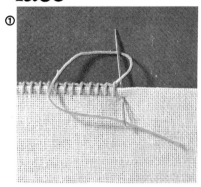

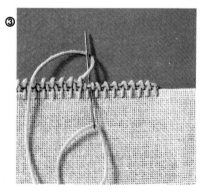

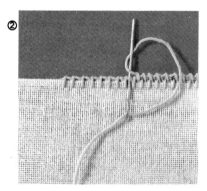

Basic method

This lace is called Puncetto in Italy and is very pretty and easy to make. It is simply needle-made knots worked in rows from left to right and back again. The best threads for this work are firm, tightly twisted yarns such as fine crochet cotton, for a chunky effect pearl cotton and Crysette can be used. Work with a blunt tapestry needle. The lace must always be worked on the right side of the fabric.

When starting, hold fabric in left hand. Work on a selvedge or make a small hem. Secure thread with a couple of tiny back stitches on wrong side of work and bring needle out on the edge. Keep stitches of the first row of equal depth and distance from each other and each knot of uniform tension (1). Working from left to right, bring needle upward under the edge of the cloth, two or three threads in from edge. Take working thread in right hand and wind it round needle once. (Take it from left to right and back, passing it in front of needle first). Pull needle up, tightening knot. Continue, making as many knots as required along edge.

(2) Work from right to left. Bring needle upwards through the space between the last two knots of preceding row. Wind thread round needle (from right to left and back, passing in front of the needle first) then pull it up, tightening knot. Continue to end of row.

(3) Repeat first and second rows as many times as required to make a solid border.

Bar lace

Work rows from left to right, fastening off thread at end of each row.

(1) Insert needle upwards. Make knots as for basic method, leaving thread loose between them to form small bars.

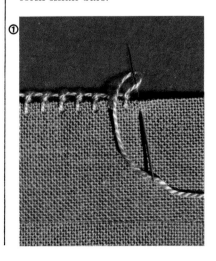

(2) Make knots and bars from left to right by inserting the needle through the previous row of bars.

(3) Repeat for depth required.

Double knot

Work from left to right, fastening off thread at end of each row. Insert the needle upwards.

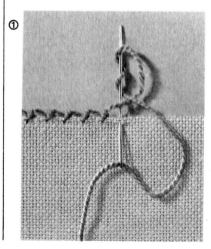

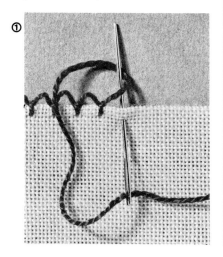

(1) Pass the thread coming from the cloth over the needle to the right. Wind the thread from the eye of the needle twice round the point from right to left. Pull needle through, tightening knot. Continue along border, leaving about 6mm ($\frac{1}{4}$in) between each stitch.

(2) Work from left to right. Insert needle through first loop and wind thread twice round needle. Pull needle through, forming a knot.

Lace arches

(1) Work from left to right making knots as in basic method but leaving thread loose between them to form small loops. A pencil or knitting needle used as a gauge will help to keep loops even. The appearance of the lace depends on this, as shown overleaf.

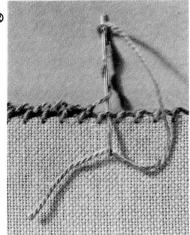

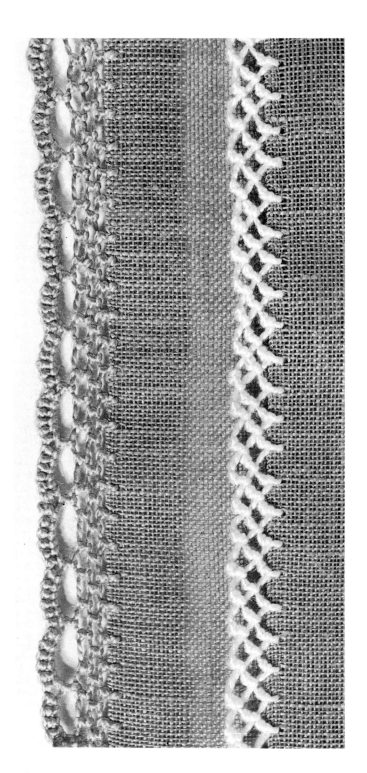

These edgings in needle-made lace are perfect for decorating handkerchiefs, table napkins or baby linen. If they are worked in a thicker thread they can also be used on guest towels, tablecloths or sheets.

N

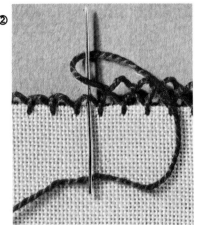

(2) Work from right to left, in the same way, using previous rows of loops as a base.

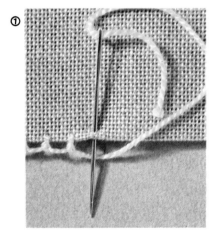

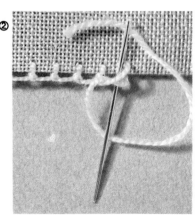

Simple lace

Hold the work downwards and work from left to right.

(1) Insert needle downwards through fabric and passing it over the thread, make a small loop or blanket stitch.

(2) Finish the loop by securing it with a knot by passing the needle from left to right through the loop and tightening it.

Aemilia-Ars lace

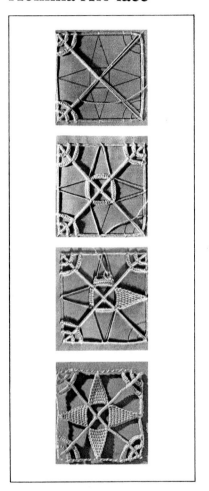

Unlike other forms of needle-made lace, most of which are built up as edgings or inserts, Aemilia-Ars lace is built up over its own skeleton lattice base which is prepared as follows: Copy design on to linen-face paper fixed to a thin card or a small piece of cardboard. Make pin-holes where lines of the motif touch the line of the surround. Using buttonhole thread, make tiny bars by threading needle through each hole and taking it outside the outline. (Make central cross for design shown).

(1) Starting at bottom right hand corner, lay thread round the edges of the square, passing thread under prepared bars. Repeat round outside edge, then lay one of the diagonals under the central cross, under the bar in the top left hand corner taking in the thread of the frame and then back to starting point. Repeat once more to make a diagonal three threads thick. Working down from corner, cover first part of diagonal in cording (wrapping thread round and round the core) as far as first cross bar. Make bar by laying a padding thread over and under the thread of the surround to left, right and left again. Work back to diagonal covering first half of bar in buttonhole stitch. Lay third padding thread as for second half of bar and then work back to centre, covering padding with buttonhole stitch. Continue cording along diagonal as far as second bar. Work bar as first. Cover diagonal in cording as far as centre. Lay part of second diagonal from here into bottom left hand corner and back to centre. Then take it out to opposite corner to lay second half, then back to bottom left hand corner. Work back to centre as for previous diagonal and cross bars. Take thread out to top right hand corner, thus laying third thread. Work corner as previous two. Complete by cording back into centre. From centre, cord along remaining diagonal until point where it crosses central square. Outline square with two padding threads and cover them in buttonhole stitch.

(2) Lay a single base thread for the star, fixing all points to surrounding square, starting with right hand point and working anti-clockwise.

(3) Points of star are filled entirely in buttonhole stitch. Work from centre outwards, decreasing one stitch on each row. Work anti-clockwise, threading through back of work to bring thread to centre after each point is completed. Now complete fourth dia-

Aemilia-Ars lace originally came from Bologna and was famous
for its delicacy and the variety of its designs. Here it is used to
decorate a tablemat and napkin, combined with satin stitch,
cording and a four-sided stitch border. To insert Aemilia-Ars
motifs into fabric, first lightly mark the outline of the lace onto the
material either in pencil or with dressmakers' carbon. Make sure
that the straight edges of the design follow the weave of the fabric.
Fix the motif in place on the outline and secure with small tacking
stitches at the centre and also round the edges. Work buttonhole
stitch or cording all round the edges of the motif. Once this is
completed, free the central tacking stitches and then cut away the
fabric within the outline.

N

gonal. Cord out from centre to corner and work pattern in same way as others.

(4) Finish framework by overcasting it. Fasten off securely, then take motif off the card by cutting small thread bars.

Ardenza lace

This type of lace is worked with a similar technique to the better-known Renaissance lace. The motifs are worked over fine braid foundations. When used to decorate household linen it is combined with cording or overcasting. The lace is named after the Italian town of its origin.

Borders

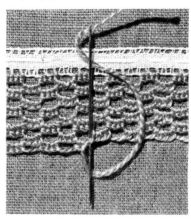

Buttonhole scallops (small)
1st row Work groups of four buttonhole stitches and loops.
2nd row As for first row, working buttonhole stitches into the loops.

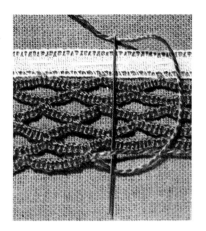

Buttonhole scallops (large)
1st row Work a row of loops.
2nd row Work over loops in buttonhole stitch.
3rd row Work loops from the centre of each preceding loop to the centre of the next and work over in buttonhole stitch. Repeat.

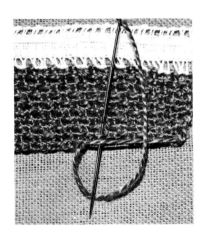

Chestnut
1st row Work groups of two buttonhole stitches.
2nd row Pass the thread from right to left as illustrated.
3rd row Make two buttonhole stitches into each loop of first row, passing needle under foundation thread applied in second row as shown.

Diagonal
1st row Work groups of three buttonhole stitches.
2nd row Pass thread from right to left as illustrated.
3rd row Work groups of three

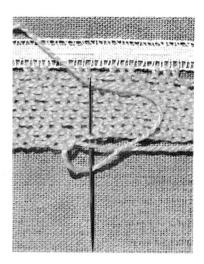

buttonhole stitches passing needle under foundation thread in previous row as shown. In each row start group of three stitches one stitch to the right so that diagonal pattern is formed.

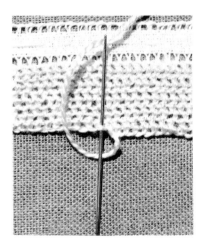

Hazel
1st row Work a row of buttonhole stitches.
2nd row Buttonhole stitch into loops of previous row. Repeat first and second rows for depth required.

Loophole
Build up basic edging to depth required, then work solid sections alternating with loopholes as follows:
(1) Work a section of knots in rows from left to right and back

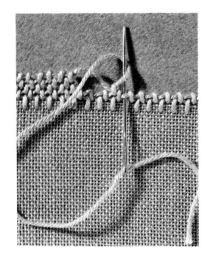

It is used in Venetian, Burano and Renaissance lace making.
(1) For the first row a twisted buttonhole stitch is used, worked from left to right.
(2) Work one overcasting stitch into loop of each stitch of previous row.

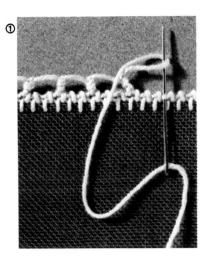

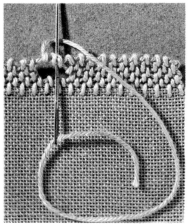

working one knot less at the end of each row. Continue until triangle is completed. Overcast along side to bring thread back to foundation line ready to start next triangle.

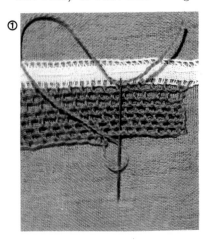

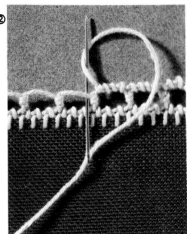

again until required depth is reached. To make loophole, miss two or three foundation knots and start a square by making a knot. Insert needle upwards through next space but before tightening it, measure out enough thread with the needle to form three sides of a small square (fourth side is provided by the base). Make knot at base of square.
(2) Work a section of knots in rows from left to right and back again to match the first. At end of each row on square side, make last knot round thread which forms third side of square. Over top of square work same number of knots as were missed at base.

Pyramid

Using basic method, work as many knots as required to form base of first triangle and then turn,

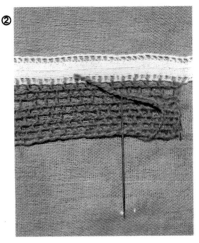

Tulle

The stitching is intended to look like the fabric of the same name.

Trellises

(1) Work from left to right. Make two rows of edging on fabric, finishing at the left. At beginning of third row start first square by missing two foundation knots and making a knot. Insert needle upwards through the next space but before tightening it, measure out enough thread with the needle to form three sides of a small square (fourth side is provided by the base). Tighten the knot and make three or four knots round

N

This pyramid border would look very pretty edging a baby's pillow or a collar and cuffs. Made up in a thicker thread and only one colour it would make an attractive trimming for a roller blind or lampshade.

the thread which forms third side, ending with needle facing upwards. Continue forming the other squares in same way, missing two knots and measuring out thread to obtain the two sides of next square. Complete row of foundation squares.

(2) Working from right to left, cover top thread of foundation squares with a row of knots, working about three knots for every square.

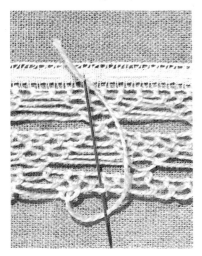

Triangles

1st row Work a row of buttonhole stitches.

2nd row Work five stitches into every six buttonhole stitches of the previous row. Continue, decreasing one stitch per group in every row so that stitches form triangles. When triangles are completed, start from beginning again.

Turkish

This border is built up on the same principle as the pyramid

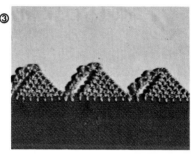

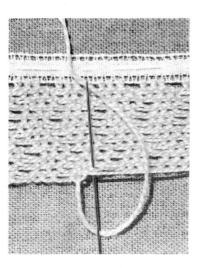

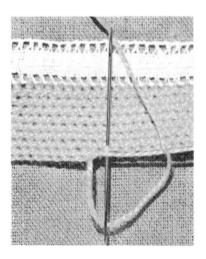

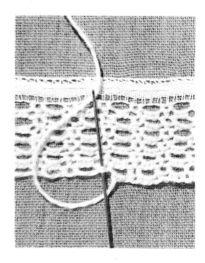

border. Twisted knots are made as shown in step (1) and worked from right to left over a foundation thread. To make the side loops, pass a thread from topmost point of triangle down to base and back to top, then work knots down it with little loops between (2) these complete this decorative border.

Vertical bars

1st row Work groups of two buttonhole stitches spaced as shown.

2nd row Work groups of three stitches into the spaces left in first row and one stitch between

the pair of buttonhole stitches. Repeat first and second rows for depth required.

Violet

1st row Work pairs of buttonhole stitches along row.

2nd row Make two buttonhole stitches into loops of previous row. Repeat first and second rows for depth required.

Yellow

1st row Work a row of button-hole stitches.

2nd row Pass thread from right to left as illustrated.

3rd row Work in buttonhole stitch into each loop of the first row, passing needle under foundation thread of previous row as shown.

Zigzag

First work buttonhole stitch in groups of three as illustrated. In the next three successive rows work the group of three stitches one stitch further to the right in each row. In the following three rows, work the group of three stitches one stitch further to the left in each row. Continue, alternating three rows of stitches worked towards the right with three rows worked towards the left, thus producing a zigzag effect.

Hedebo

This work originated in Denmark and is easily executed. Areas to be filled are cut out and raw edges turned under and worked with a row of basic edging. Spaces are then filled with a variety of buttonhole bars and pyramids while centre is worked with a circle of bar lace.

N

Renaissance

A delicate Italian needle-made lace based on a foundation of ready made braid which outlines the motifs and edges, these are twisted into flower and leaf shapes then filled and joined by a groundwork of bars which are also decorated according to taste.

Web motif

First prepare foundation border with several rows of basic edging. Begin the web with a left to right row.

1st row Work four knots, miss two foundation knots forming the thread into a loop over them. Work one knot into the next one. Cover right hand side of loop with knots, bringing needle out at top. Miss two more foundation knots and once again looping the thread, make one knot into the next one. Make four more knots (1).

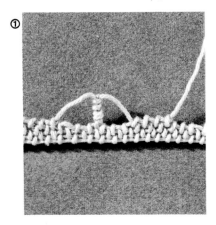

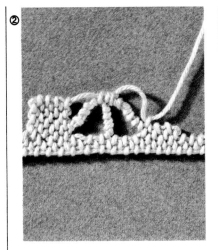

2nd row Working from right to left, make four knots, cover the two loops with knots, then end with four knots.

3rd row Working from left to right, make four knots and work backwards and forward over these

until the work is high enough for the threads to be laid for horizontal bar of web. Make a bar across to the central column and fasten in the centre with three knots. Work rest of bar leaving thread loose (2) so that right hand rows from left to right and back can be worked, taking in the thread as well, up to the level of the horizontal bar. Finish with a complete row from right to left, making knots on the horizontal bars.

Work rows backwards and forwards over the first four knots. Then fasten thread in centre with two knots to form a loop. Leave another loop and work several rows on the right hand knots to build up level with left (3). Next row, working from right to left, cover loops with knots. Next row, working from left to right, work four knots then fasten thread to centre of web to form central column. Work up this with three or four knots. Make second half of the loop and work the last four knots.

Go back over the loops with a row of knots (4) and then work backwards and forwards to border top side of web.

Needles

Always use the correct needle for your work to ensure ease, comfort and good results.

For embroidery: Sharps needle, medium length with small eye, for sewing with cotton or a single strand of stranded cotton. Crewel needle (sizes 6 to 8) long and sharp with large eye, for stranded cotton, *coton à broder*, pearl cotton no 8 (size 5) larger eye, for tapestry wool and pearl cotton no.5. Chenille needle (no.19) short and sharp with large eye, for thick threads, tapestry wool, soft embroidery cotton. Tapestry needle, blunt end, for whipped and laced stitches, canvas

N

work, drawn fabric and drawn thread work. Beading needle, fine for sewing on beads. Tambour hook, similar to a crochet hook, for attaching beads.

For canvas work: use tapestry needles with large eyes and blunt points, sizes 18 to 21 are popular, use size 14 for very coarse material,
For sewing: size 8 for dressmaking, size 9 for bead embroidery and sewing fine fabrics such as silks and chiffons, size 7 for heavier sewing such as stitching on buttons. Either medium length sharps or long straw needles can be used.

Netting
Materials

You will need ordinary cotton string, coloured string or macramé-type twine. Netting needles made of plastic to hold the string are made in small, medium and large sizes. A mesh stick, ideally of perspex is used to determine the size of the mesh and ensure that meshes are all of equal size. A toggle, to suspend circular netting for bags so that it rotates freely can be made from a trouser button. As a working base, use a small weighted cushion or a brick covered with several layers of flannel.

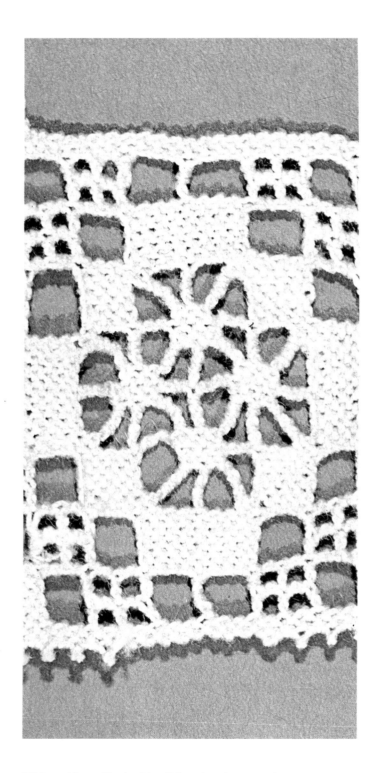

Web motifs combined with solid sections in geometric arrangements can be built up into a square insertions or borders as shown here, to suit the particular article you have in mind, particularly household linen.

N

Basic netting

To load the needle cut length of string required. Hold needle in left hand with point upwards. Hold end of string on body of needle with left thumb. Run string up the body, round prong and down same side of body to trap the starting end of the string. Take string round bottom of needle between the two projections. Turn needle back to front, still with point upwards and repeat the process.

To practise netting knot, cut two pieces of string, each about 46cm (18in) long. Tie one piece into a loop and attach with safety pin to your working base as a foundation loop. Using second piece of string, pass all except last 5cm (2in) through from back of foundation loop and hold at intersection with thumb and one

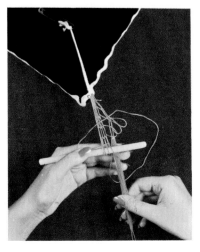

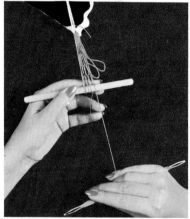

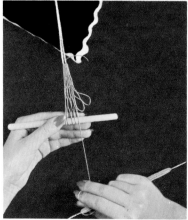

finger of left hand. Holding long end of string in right hand, throw an open loop over to left. With right hand, take end of string to right across front of foundation loop, round back and out to front through the thrown loop. Keeping left thumb and finger firmly in position until last moment, pull knot firm.

To work a piece of netting, make a foundation loop 46cm (18in) long. Load 5.5metres (6yd) of string on to needle. Fasten foundation loop to working base and attach string to bottom of foundation loop with a netting knot. **1st row** Hold mesh stick from below with left hand, thumb at the front. Lay working string over front of mesh stick, taking it round below and up behind stick and out through foundation loop from the back. Pull needle downwards with right hand and the mesh stick will be hauled by pulley effect hard up to bottom of foundation loop. With left hand thumb at front and index finger at back, hold string and foundation loop where they cross at top of mesh stick. Form knot and draw it firm. Mesh stick remains in position, encircled by this first loop and held in left hand. Needle and working string should automatically be over the front of mesh stick and ready to continue by repeating process. Knot must always be made close to top of mesh stick, otherwise meshes will not be uniform. Keeping mesh stick in position with left hand, repeat twice so there are three loops on mesh stick.
2nd row Remove mesh stick. With left hand turn the three newly made loops so that the last made loop is on the left ready to be used in the second row. As before, form loop round mesh stick and knot first loop. Take care not to include the descending strand on the left as well as the two strands of first loop. To avoid this, hold intersection with thumb and second finger of left hand and use left index finger to mark the space between the descending strand and first loop, the space in fact through which needle will pass as it comes round back of loop.
Third and subsequent rows Remove mesh stick only at end of each row and continue meshing successive rows, always working left to right.

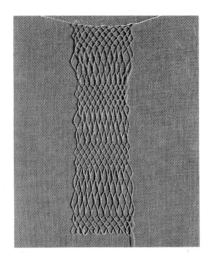

Alternating mesh

This is a very easy pattern because it consists of alternating some rows of stitches made with a small mesh stick with others worked with a larger mesh stick. Although it is quite decorative on its own an additional border of close buttonhole stitch or double crochet using the same thread as the net may be worked as a finish.

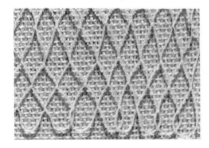

Diamond mesh

This pattern is worked in rows. Cast on mesh for first row into foundation loop working as many stitches as you will need for the net you are making (it is always the stitches that lie underneath one another that are counted). When first row of stitches is completed, slip out mesh stick and work another row of stitches into loops left in previous row.

Releasing mesh

When net is completed, pull out foundation loop and unpick cast-on knots. This means that the knots of the first row of meshes are freed and the meshes made

Netting can be delicate looking as well as hard-wearing, as seen in this table centre worked in circular netting with mesh in varying widths.

N

larger than those of succeeding rows. Therefore, for the first row, use a fractionally smaller mesh stick than that used for rest of work.

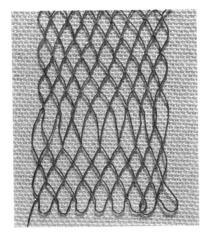

Wide mesh

To obtain a stitch which is much longer than the others, make a double loop by winding the thread twice around the mesh stick before making the knot which fastens it. In this way you can vary the pattern in alternating rows.

Netting shapes

Circular netting

Cast required number of stitches on to a foundation loop. For second row, pull up stitches to close circle, do not turn work, but knot thread into first stitch without forming a loop. Increase by working two knots into loops of previous row where required to keep work flat. Slip out mesh stick from time to time as it is difficult to work with too many stitches on it but always leave three to four stitches on mesh stick. You can net several stitches into one stitch in previous row and then draw them together by netting several stitches together so as to form a hole. Decrease by netting into each alternate stitch. By these means and by using different widths of mesh stick you can produce different patterns.

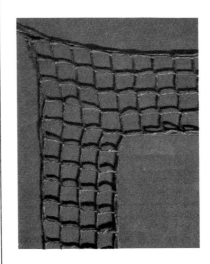

Corner

Work as for rectangle and continue until you have two stitches more than double the number of stitches required for the width of the border. Then work on half the stitches, turn and continue, alternating one row with an increase at the end of the row with another with a decrease. Fasten off as for rectangle and work remainder in the same way.

Rectangle

Work as for square until one side is width required. At the end of the following row, decrease one stitch, then continue by alternating an increase row with a

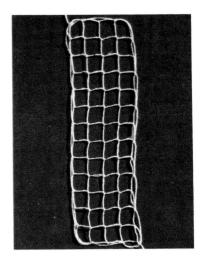

decrease row, in this way the width will remain constant. When strip is long enough, decrease one stitch at end of every row until you fasten off.

Square

Start as for making a triangle and continue until you have one more stitch than is required for the side of the square. Make one row without increasing, then start decreasing by meshing the last two loops together. Continue in this fashion until only two stitches remain. Finish by tying these two together with a netting knot.

Triangle

This net is worked diagonally. Cast on two mesh into foundation loop, remove mesh stick and turn work (netting is always worked

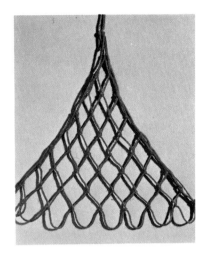

from left to right). Increase by netting two stitches into last loop of every row. Continue in this way until you obtain the desired width, adding to each row one stitch made in the last stitch of the previous row.

Norwegian embroidery

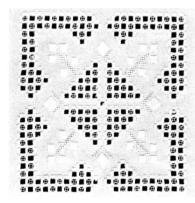

This is worked in pearl cotton on hardanger fabric or fine linen with an even weave, no.5 pearl cotton is used for the thick satin stitch blocks which are typical of this work and the finer no.8 for the woven bars and fillings. After the edges of the design have been completed the threads are cut with very sharp scissors and withdrawn. The work can then be further decorated with bars or eyelets.

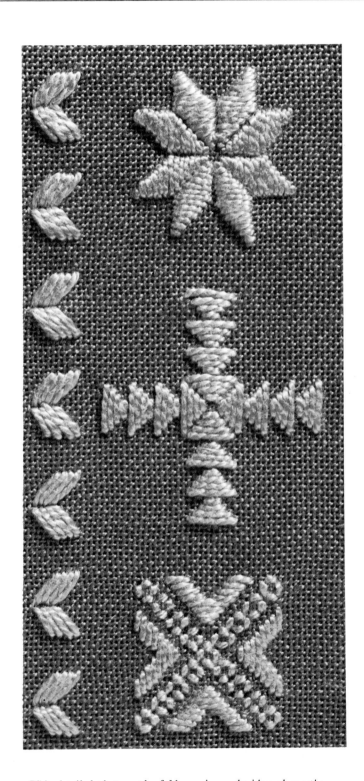

This detailed photograph of Norwegian embroidery shows the typically Scandinavian star and snowflake motifs, worked in thick blocks of satin stitch and reversed four sided stitch on even-weave fabric.

O

Openings

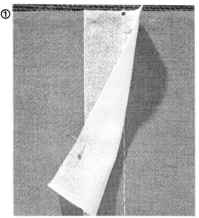

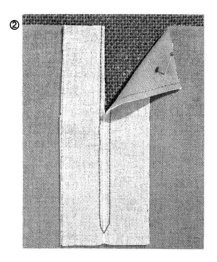

Faced

First, make a tacked line along grain of fabric to mark position and length of slit. Cut a piece of fabric about 2.5cm (1in) longer than intended opening and 6.5cm ($2\frac{1}{2}$in) wide. This piece is cut in fabric matching that of garment (shown in contrast in illustration for clarity). Mark centre of facing with tacking. With right sides together, place facing on fabric, matching lines of tacking (1). Tack round slit and machine stitch about 3mm ($\frac{1}{8}$in) each side of central line, tapering to a point at the end. (2). Cut down centre, turn facing through to right side and tack flat. Neaten raw edges with a narrow machine stitched hem, rounding corners. Slip stitch or hem facing to garment. If fabric is thin and stitches liable to

show, machine stitch round opening on right side.

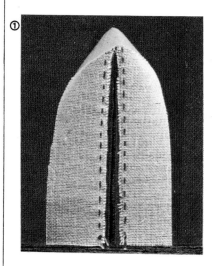

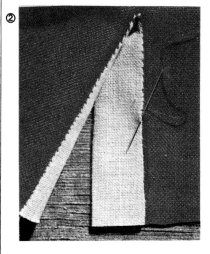

Continuous

Mark position and length of slit. Cut a lengthwise strip of fabric, twice length of opening and about 5cm (2in) wide (shown in contrast in illustration for clarity). Cut along line marked for placket. With right sides together, place facing strip to garment. Tack round slit (1) and machine stitch. Taper stitching to point at top of slit and hold slit vertically open when you come to second side so that you sew in a straight line. Turn strip to wrong side of garment and hem free edge in position (2). Press, overlapping the two sides of facing. Top of opening can be strengthened by

working a tiny buttonhole bar on right side.

Overcast stitch

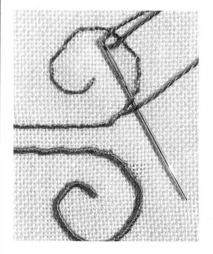

First work a row of regular running stitches along the line of the design, then work back, filling in the empty spaces left in the first line.

Work a line of overcasting over these running stitches without picking up fabric to even out any irregularities, then work a second line of closely worked overcasting without picking up fabric beneath to produce the rich corded effect.

Overcasting

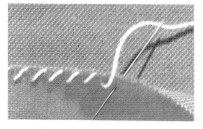

After seams have been stitched and pressed, they must be neatened to prevent fraying. Edges can be overcast by hand as shown or by using the zigzag stitch on a sewing machine.

Overcast stitch, which is found in Tuscan embroidery, is generally combined with satin stitch and four sided stitch. The working technique, given opposite, allows it to be used on loosely woven fabrics.

Palestrina, double knot stitch

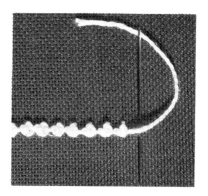

Make a small diagonal stitch over the line of design, bring needle back and slip it under the thread once, then again under the same thread making a buttonhole loop stitch. When this stitch is worked closely together it gives an attractive bold line.

Paris stitch

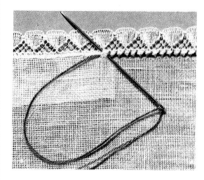

Turn up seam or hem allowance plus the depth of the lace on edge to be trimmed. Tack lace along the folded edge and work from right to left. Bring needle out to right side, picking up edge of lace, then through to wrong side picking up a few threads of fabric. Take needle back to where it came out the first time (see picture) and left for next stitch. Trim away surplus fabric on wrong side when lace is secured.

P

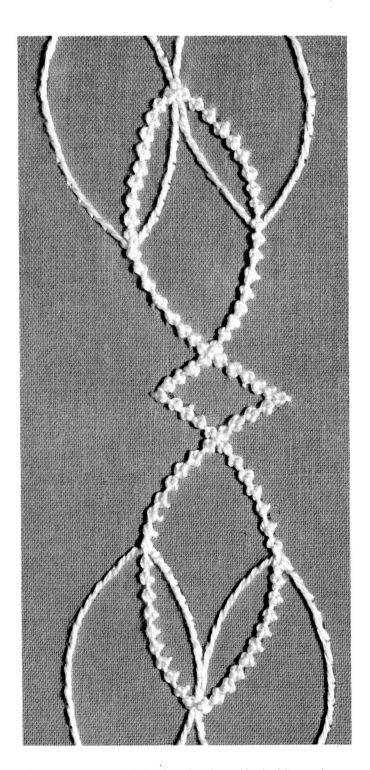

The textured look of Palestrina stitch is combined with smooth stem stitch for a simple outline design. It is generally worked in a light shade to contrast with a darker fabric, or vice versa.

Parma braid

First work three rows of chain stitch running closely side by side and in the same direction, with the chains level. On curves it is important to make the stitches smaller on the inside of a curve and slightly longer on the outer edge to keep the chains level. Next work two rows of blanket stitch over the chain stitch, without picking up the fabric. The knotted edges of the blanket stitches lie towards the centre giving a raised braid effect.

Patchwork

Materials
The best materials for patchwork are those which do not fray or stretch, and are firm in weave and texture

Always observe two important rules when selecting materials for a piece of work Never mix silks and cottons and only combine materials of equal weight and thickness.

You will also need:
Templates: made from metal, perspex or very stiff card, the exact size of finished patch.

Stiff paper: for the paper shapes which are tacked into the pieces of fabric to hold the patches firm. These shapes must be very accurately cut.

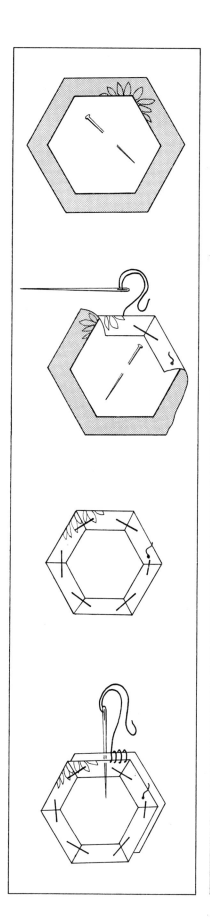

An eternal interlocking pattern in Parma braid embroidery. This technique is ideal for working on a large scale on curtains or wall hangings; in finer thread it makes a striking decoration for cushions.

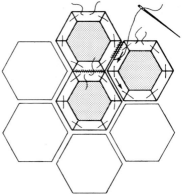

Hexagons, making up a rosette, these are the simplest shapes for beginners

Sharp pencil: scissors, sharp for fabric, old for paper, fine needle and steel pins; fine sewing cotton for cotton fabrics, silk for silk; mercerised cotton for tacking.

Making the patches
Using the template draw round with sharp pencil and carefully cut out the paper shapes Press fabric if creased, then using the template as a guide cut out the patches, allowing 1cm (⅜in) extra for turnings. Try to keep the two edges of the template parallel to the grain of the fabric as this strengthens the patch. Pin the paper shape on to the wrong side of the fabric and fold over the turnings. Starting with a knot or back stitch, tack round the patch, using one tacking stitch to hold down each corner. Finish off by making a small extra stitch to hold down each corner and take out pin.

Flowered and checked patchwork for a breakfast set and a matching cushion

Joining the patches
Put the right sides of two patches together and oversew with tiny stitches along one edge. Start by laying end of thread along top of edge and sew over it from right to left. Push the needle through fabric at right angles to edge so that stitches will be neat and patches will not stretch.
To fasten off, work backwards for four stitches. Make sure corners are firm by sewing extra stitches over them. Sew together small units first and join up these groups later when you can plan the finished effect to your satisfaction. Press on wrong side with warm iron.

Finishing patchwork
The tacking and papers are all removed when the patches have been joined. But edges may need to be straightened by inserting half patches, or strips may be placed behind to fill spaces or strengthen curves. The work needs to be lined to strengthen and neaten, once straightened, edges can be bound, piped or corded to give a good finish.

Pekinese

First work a foundation of small back stitches, then loop a second thread through the stitches as shown. Two colours or thicknesses of threads can be used.

Piping

Choose a piping cord suitable for purpose and fabric being used. Cut a length of bias fabric wide enough to fold round cord, plus turnings, and long enough to pipe whole seam. Fold strip round cord, right side outside, and sew with running stitch close to cord. Seam can be worked as a lapped seam as shown. Fold turnings under on top section of article. If seam is shaped, turnings must be snipped so that they lie flat. Place hem fold close to piping, pin and tack. Place this section over the under-piece, with inner edge of piping to fitting line. Pin, tack and sew with slip hemming or by machine. On a straight seam, tack covered piping to right side of one edge of article, raw edges together. Place second section of article over this so that piping is enclosed along fitting line and sew with machine stitching. Turn to right side.

Pisan embroidery

The technique used is similar to that for working eyelets, with the addition of overcast bars. To prepare, fabric must be tacked on to linen-face paper. Eyelets are

P

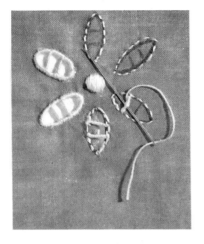

outlined with little running stitches before overcasting and the bars are worked without picking up any of the fabric below. When completed, fabric is cut away carefully and the cut edges overcast again on the wrong side.

Pleats

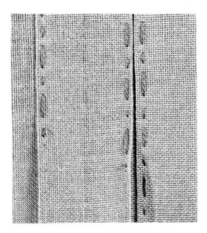

Box

These are broad flat pleats on the right side of the garment, with two edges meeting down the centre on the back. Amount of fabric required for a skirt is roughly three times hip measurement plus turnings. Each pleat must be carefully measured and marked so that all are of equal depth. Before fabric is cut it is essential that edges are straight on the grain, to do this draw a thread out from the raw edge of

the fabric and cut along the line made by the thread. When pleats are measured and folded to the required depth, pin and tack in position using long and short tacking stitches. Six lines of tacking are needed for each pleat, down the two front folds, the centre folds on the wrong side and the line where the front folds lie on each side.

Flat

These pleats are all turned in one direction. Straighten grain of fabric as for box pleats, the same amount of fabric is needed. Three lines of tacking are needed for each pleat, marking front and back edges and a line for the edge of the front fold.

It is helpful to use a contrasting coloured thread for this as shown.

Pockets

One-piece bound

This is made with a similar technique to a bound buttonhole. First, cut pocket section to required depth and width. Mark position of pocket opening on garment and on pocket section. With right sides together, place pocket on garment, matching marking lines. Using running stitch mark a rectangle outlining

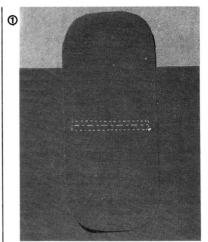
①

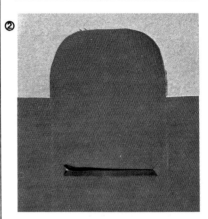
②

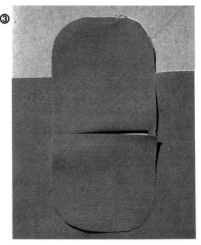
③

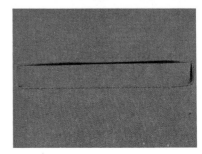

174

P

pocket about 1cm ($\frac{3}{8}$in) away from central line (1).

Machine stitch around marked rectangle. Cut along line of opening to within 1cm ($\frac{3}{8}$in) from ends, then diagonally to corners (2). Pull pocket to wrong side through opening. Turn seams away from opening, bringing folded edges together (3) so that tiny inverted pleats are formed at the ends. Keep lips of pocket binding even. Tack in position. (Pocket can be finished on right side by stitching round opening, close to binding). On wrong side, pin upper section of pocket to lower section. Stitch around edge and overcast to neaten.

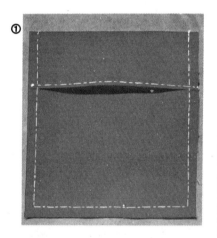

Patch

Mark position of pocket on garment. Cut out pocket to size required, adding about 4cm (1$\frac{1}{2}$in)

to depth for top facing and 1cm ($\frac{3}{8}$in) seam allowances all round. Turn under seam allowance along upper edge and stitch. Fold top facing to right side and stitch to pocket at sides (1). Trim seams and turn back to wrong side.

Clip seam allowance below fold, turn under seam allowance round sides and base of pocket and tack. Topstitch or hem to garment, fastening off top corners securely because they will have to stand a lot of strain. If fabric is thin it is best to underlay these spots with a small piece of fabric before attaching pocket, this strengthens the fabric. If a self flap is required for pocket, simply cut top facing deeper to allow for this and turn over to front when attaching pocket.

Patch pocket with flap

Make patch pocket as before. Cut out pocket flap, making it about 3mm ($\frac{1}{8}$in) wider than pocket at each side and about one third depth of pocket. Two pieces will be needed for flap, one in fabric being used for garment and a second section in lining. With right sides together, place flap to lining and stitch round sides, leaving lower edge open. Trim turnings, turn to right side and press. Place flap, face down on right side of garment with raw edge level with top of pocket and

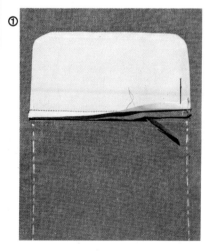

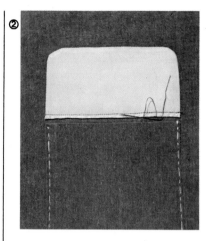

stitch. Trim seam allowance of top of flap only, leaving lining (1). Turn under edge of lining and hem to garment (2). Turn flap down over pocket.

Press studs

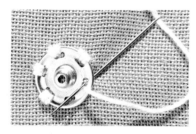

Sew on ball section first to upper part of garment opening. Press against lower section of opening leaving a tiny mark to show position for socket of press stud. Oversew into one hole two or three times passing the needle under the stud to the next hole until each hole has been firmly stitched.

Q

Quill stitch

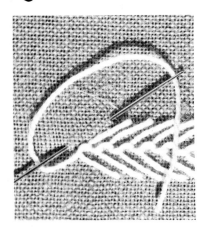

Work from right to left. Bring needle through on centre line of design. Make a long, slightly sloping back stitch, bring needle through again, a little in front of previous stitch, catching the working thread under needle. Repeat, taking the back stitch alternately to either side of centre line of design to form a quill.

Quilting

Traditional
This is the simplest form of quilting where the complete surface is padded. Terylene wadding is placed between the top fabric and the backing fabric and all

A slim and elegant quilted dressing gown with a nightie in matching fabric

three layers are stitched together by machine or by hand using running stitch. The conventional motif is the diamond, but other geometric forms or gentle curves can be used. The work can be stitched on the wrong side if the design needs to be marked on paper as for a quilt, but usually the work is carried out on the right side.

Italian

Instead of being padded all over, only the outlines of the design are padded to give a raised or corded effect. The transfer or design used must be one especially intended for this type of quilting, or bold appliqué designs can be used by drawing a double outline about 6mm ($\frac{1}{4}$in) or less inside the original design line. Designs are generally applied to the top fabric rather than the lining and stitched by hand using either a 'small back stitch or running stitch worked in sewing cotton or pure silk. Pad the double lines of stitching by threading with either 8 ply wool, rug wool or quilting wool, using a tapestry needle. The backing fabric must be open weave, such as muslin, so that the needle carrying the padding thread can come out through it and be inserted again following the curve of the design, leaving a small loop each time needle is inserted in fabric.

The narrow padded lines of Italian quilting can be used to make a pretty decoration for bed or cot covers, cushions or evening bags.

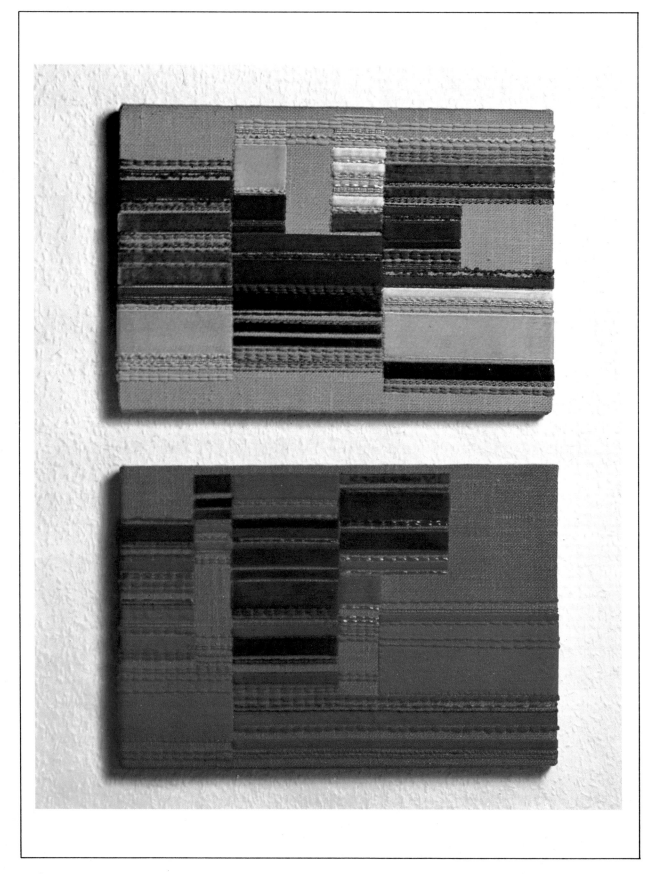

Ribbon embroidery

This is a simple form of appliqué. The decoration is stitched in place with sewing cotton, invisible sewing thread or embroidery thread if the ribbon is held down with a decorative stitch. Background fabric should be firmly woven, such as velvet, furnishing fabric or strong linen. Designs should be basically simple, detail can be added in the form of embroidery stitches or beading. To work, first trace design on to fabric. Stitch outline braid round design using small running stitch or back stitch, ease round corners. Flowers are made by looping ribbon into shape of individual petals and securing ends of loops with several stitches. For ears of corn work a line of double loops, going to right and left of a central stem, stitching loops down centre as you work.

Roses

Cut a piece of bias fabric about 60cm (24in) long and 6cm (2¼in) wide. Vary the dimensions according to size of flower or bud re-

Geometric interpretation, using various widths of velvet ribbon mounted on heavy dress linen

quired. Fold fabric in half lengthwise, wrong sides together (1). Run a gathering thread through both layers of fabric. Draw up the gathering thread, beginning to coil rosebud at the same time (2). Coil tightly to begin with, gradually making the coils looser to form the shape of the flower. Fold over end and sew doubled edges to lower edge of rose. Cut leaf shapes from bias fabric, these can be reinforced with extra fabric glued to the back with fabric adhesive. Alternatively, leaf can be made in two layers, stitched with wrong sides together leaving small gap for turning, then turned right side out and neatened. Rose can be finished with a small stem made

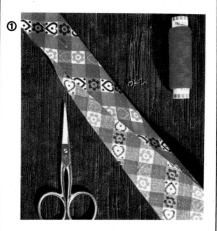

First fold the fabric strip lengthwise with the wrong sides together

Run a gathering thread close to raw edge, draw up, coiling the flower

Finished flowers and leaves, these can also be made in plain organdie

from a rouleau of fabric (3). To make this, cut a narrow bias strip, fold in half lengthwise, stitch with right sides together along edge and pull through to right side.

Rug making
Short pile method

This technique is worked with a blunt-ended rug needle over a short-pile gauge which is a piece of plastic, metal or wood about 1cm (⅜in) wide. The Turkey canvas used is made in a range of widths which can easily be joined if necessary and the rug wool is used in skeins, not cut lengths.

R

179

R

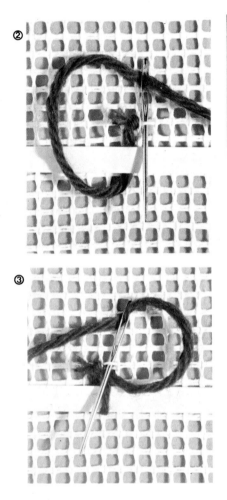

② ③

Work as follows:

(1) Insert needle under lower canvas thread, then under top thread. Bring needle over looped wool to form a knot.

(2) Lay gauge on canvas, passing wool under and over gauge.

(3) Insert needle under lower canvas thread with wool to left of needle, then insert needle under upper canvas thread with wool to right of needle. Move gauge along as work proceeds.

When work is completed, wool can either be cut or left in loops to vary the texture. Carpet braid can be used for binding or facing raw edges of canvas, this is stitched with linen thread. Otherwise edges can be bound with matching wool using binding stitch. To work this, thread needle with wool, bring through from back of canvas, over selvedge edge from first to fourth hole, then back to second hole. Continue, working forward to fifth hole, back to third hole and so on.

Once you have mastered the technique, you can work your own simple designs, marking the canvas with a felt-tipped pen or buy a canvas already stencilled with the pattern.

Rumanian stitch

This filling stitch can be used in many ways to give different effects. It can be worked between two parallel lines as shown, either straight or curved, with the stitches placed closely together. For shading, stitches are worked with slight spaces in between and the next row of stitches worked into the spaces. It is also useful for filling in leaf or petal shapes. Work from left to right. Bring needle out on right side of work and, keeping thread on right, insert needle 15 threads above, bring needle out 5 threads below this point and keeping thread over needle, re-insert needle another 5 threads below, bringing it out very near first point. Continue until required area is filled. The centre crossing stitch can be varied to make a longer slanting stitch or a small straight stitch for different fillings.

Running stitch

This is worked horizontally from right to left. Pass the needle over and under the fabric, making upper stitches the same length and the under ones half as long (also keeping them the same length as each other). Running stitches of varying lengths can be worked in rows to build up a regular pattern. This is known as pattern darning. Even-weave fabrics such as linen or wool are suitable fabrics for this work stitched with stranded or pearl cotton for towels, table cloths or napkins and tapestry wool for woollen fabrics. Pattern darning can also be done on knitted garments or very loose tweeds using narrow velvet ribbon.

Running stitch, long and short

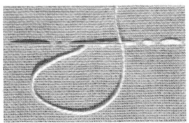

Work as for running stitch but make the upper stitches alternately long and short, the short ones being equal in length to the stitches underneath.

R

A striking sunflower rug, shown here as a wall hanging. Worked on a smaller scale it could be backed and filled and used as a floor cushion. The design is simple enough for a beginner to tackle and the motif can be used in a variety of ways. A rectangular rug could be made with a design of six sunflower heads, symmetrically arranged and an entirely different look could be achieved by including the stems and leaves, radiating from the centre of a circular rug.

S

S

Satin stitch

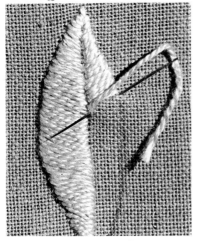

This consists of straight stitches worked evenly and closely together and is useful for solid fillings. However, if working this stitch for any article likely to be frequently handled it is unwise to use a stitch more than 1cm ($\frac{3}{8}$in) long, because it will not wear well. When using a twisted yarn such as pearl cotton, take care to keep it evenly twisted while working. Stranded cotton is more difficult to use successfully as all the strands must lie flat and parallel.

Satin stitch, padded

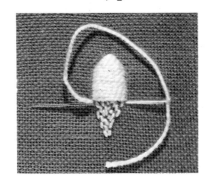

First outline shape with small running stitches, fill in outline with more running stitches (chain stitch or stem stitch are also suitable for padding) and then cover with satin stitch.

Embroidery from a matador's cloak in padded satin stitch on silk

Satin stitch, double padding

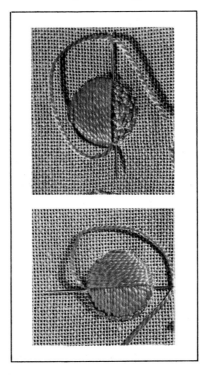

Worked when more pronounced padding is required. (1) Fill in shape with running stitches and cover with satin stitch in one direction, then work over the same area again at right angles to the first row of stitching.

Seams

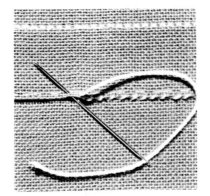

Flat fell

With right sides together, stitch fabric along line of seam. Trim one edge of seam close to seam line. Turn under wider edge, pin and tack over trimmed seam allowance. Machine stitch close to edge or hem by hand.

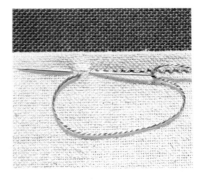

French

This is a double seam with the raw edges encased, it is suitable for use on sheer fabrics. First, with wrong sides together, pin, tack and machine stitch seam 3mm ($\frac{1}{8}$in) from edge. Turn garment to wrong side and stitch on original seam line, encasing the raw edges in the seam. (Illustration shows optional hand stitching).

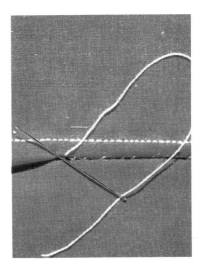

Hemmed fell

This seam is worked similarly to flat fell, but on wrong side of garment. Place right sides of fabric together for first line of machine stitching, then hem folded edge in place by hand.

183

S

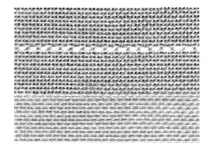

Plain

Easiest and most frequently used seam. Right sides of fabric are placed together with edges meeting. Seam is pinned, tacked and stitched by machine or by hand. A plain seam is usually pressed open and finished according to the fabric used. Edges can be overcast by hand either singly or together if seam is pressed in one direction, edges can also be zigzag stitched or overcast by machine, stitched flat, pinked or bound Seams in dressmaking are usually sewn by machine, but hand sewing gives an exquisite finish to baby clothes or fine lingerie

Seeding

This simple filling is made up of many small straight stitches of equal length placed at random. Seeding can be used to fill any area and to give a textured effect to a design. For a more pronounced effect two stitches can be worked over each other.

Shadow work

This is of oriental origin and is traditionally worked entirely in white threads on white semi-transparent fabric although modern interpretations favour working with a single colour thread on a matching or strongly contrasting background. It is best reserved for articles which receive little wear. The stitch used in shadow work is called double back stitch or herringbone, the crossed threads lie at the back of the work so that they show through the transparent fabric and the back stitches lie on the surface as an outline. Designs can be transferred to either the wrong side or right side of the fabric, depending on whether you choose to work the design from the back or the front. (If other stitches are being used on the surface for detail it will be more convenient to work from the right side so that progress can be observed without constantly turning work

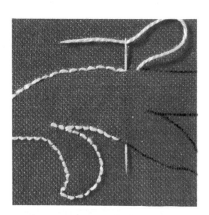

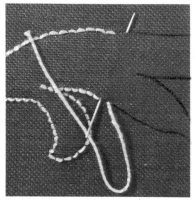

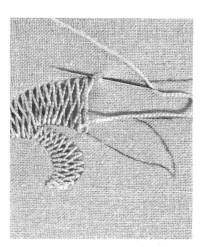

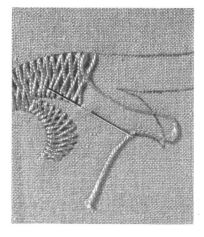

over). An embroidery frame is advisable to prevent stitches pulling and causing puckering.

Transparent or very fine fabrics are essential because the filling stitches must show through to create the opaque shadow effect. Organdie, lawn, nylon chiffon and muslin are all suitable fabrics. Fine yarns such as stranded cotton or pure stranded silk are recommended for the embroidery. First pictures show first stages of working double back stitch from the front. When working round a curve the back stitches on the inside must be smaller than on the outside curve. The third and fourth pictures show the double back stitch being worked on wrong side of fabric.

Flowers to embroider in shadow work: this full-sized design could be traced.

184

Sheaf stitch

This filling is made from groups of four satin stitches which are caught down with a straight stitch across the centre, making a sheaf shape. In illustration it is shown combined with satin stitch worked in pearl cotton on even weave linen.

Shirring

A form of decorative gathering in which several rows of gathers are made one under the other and equal distances apart. These rows are visible and provide an attractive soft effect when worked on sheer fabric. Space running stitches very evenly, in rows about 6mm ($\frac{1}{4}$in) apart. Begin about 4 or 5mm ($\frac{3}{16}$in) above the fitting line and then work as many rows as required. Draw up all the rows together to width required, wind

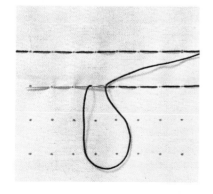

Elastic yarn is used to shir the waist and sleeves of this little girl's dress.

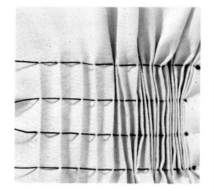

ends round a pin while arranging fullness regularly. Fasten off securely on wrong side.

This method is also used when making normal gathers. Work two rows of running stitch, draw up to required size, machine stitch to secure, then remove gathering threads.

Shirring can also be worked by machine with elastic yarn to give self-adjusting gathers Most modern machines carry instructions for using shirring yarns.

Siennese stitch

This is worked between straight or curved parallel lines. It can also be used as a filling stitch, the width of the bars varying to fit the outline. To begin, work one vertical stitch, bring needle out a few threads to the right, make

loop as for buttonhole stitch, picking up thread of first stitch but not fabric beneath, re-insert needle on top line and continue as shown.

Slav embroidery

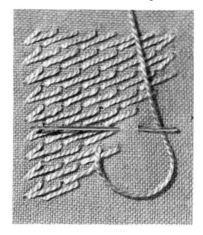

Diagonal
A line or filling stitch worked on counted threads. Work diagonally from left to right, taking needle 8 threads along and 4 threads up for each stitch, then bring out needle 4 threads to left. Continue with stitches of equal size. Finish row with a short stitch taken 4 threads to left.

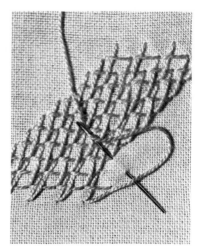

Diagonal (crossed)
Work diagonally upwards from

S

left to right, insert needle 12 threads up and 6 threads to the right, bring it out 6 threads below, next insert needle 6 threads above initial stitch and out again at starting point. Continue in same way, crossing one diagonal and one horizontal stitch.

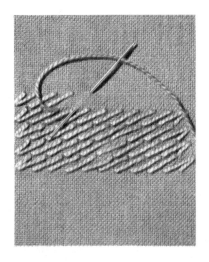

Horizontal

Worked in the same way as diagonal Slav, but in horizontal lines instead of diagonal.

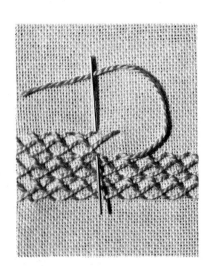

Horizontal (crossed)

Work from left to right. Starting at left hand corner, insert needle 8 threads up to the left, then bring needle out 8 threads below, re-insert needle 16 threads to right and 8 threads up, out again 8 threads below.

Smocking

The basis of smocking is the gathering which forms the pleats, once this is worked a variety of decorative stitches can be applied. Smooth, even-textured fabrics are most suitable, cottons, silks or fine woollens. Fine fabrics such as voile and lawn are exquisite when smocked, but need more practice. *Coton à broder* or pearl cotton are ideal yarns for smocking embroidery.

It is essential to keep smocking pleats even and regular and for this purpose transfers for smocking dots can be used. Dots from 6mm ($\frac{1}{4}$in) to 1cm ($\frac{3}{8}$in) are suitable for most fabrics.

As a rough guide, fabric before smocking should measure about three times required finished width. Smocking should be worked before the garment is sewn together. Use smocking to smarten babies' and children's angel tops and dresses—front and back—and cuffs.

Step by step

(1) Cut transfer to length and depth required and iron it on to wrong side of fabric. Beginning at first right hand dot, on wrong side of fabric, secure thread firmly with a knot and a back stitch. Work from right to left and carefully pick up each dot along the line leaving a short length of thread hanging loose at end of

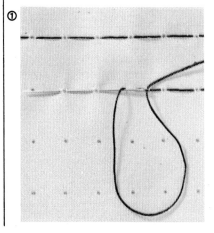

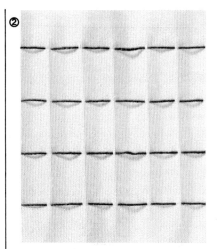

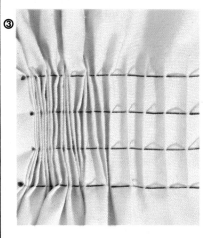

row.

(2) Repeat until all the rows are completed.

(3) Pull all the threads together, not too tightly. Knot ends together in pairs, sliding knot along thread on a pin and cut threads to within 5cm (2in) of the knots. Leave gathering threads in place and remove them when smocking is completed. Use gathering lines as a guide to keep smocking stitches straight. Dotted, striped or checked fabrics may not need gathering transfers as the pattern of the fabric itself can be used as a guide, but it is important to decide which area of the pattern is required on the surface of the finished smocking.

Traditional smocks are embroidered to indicate the wearer's trade: this little boy wears cartwheels on his collar.

S

Cable stitch

This is a firm control stitch and two rows worked closely together at top and bottom of a band of smocking prevent the piece from spreading too much. It can be used as a single line or in several rows worked closely together between rows of freer stitches to give strength to a design.

Work from left to right. Join thread to left of first pleat, pass needle over two pleats and insert from right to left under second pleat, bringing it out between the two and keeping thread below needle. Make a stitch into next pleat, from right to left, with thread above needle. Repeat these two movements to end of row.

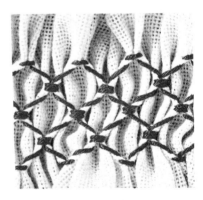

Diamond

Care should be taken not to make this stitch too large or finished smocking will lack firmness. It is worked from left to right in two stages and each stage is worked between two rows of gathering threads. Join thread to first pleat on second line of running stitch, then pick up second pleat, from right to left, with thread below

needle. Pass to first line of running stitch above, pick up third pleat from right to left, then fourth, keeping thread above needle. Move down to second line and pick up fifth pleat, from right to left. Continue to end of work, then work a second line to complete diamonds as illustrated.

Double feather

This is a fairly tight stitch which is worked like ordinary feather stitch, picking up a pleat of the fabric for each stitch and working from right to left. It needs a little practice to achieve the even effect needed for smocking.

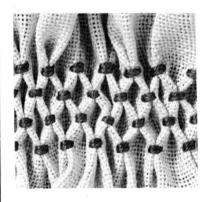

Honeycomb

This is a medium control stitch and is worked from left to right. Bring needle up at top of first pleat and make a back stitch picking up the next pleat on the right. Take a second back stitch, slipping needle down through pleat and bring it to the right ready to make the next double back stitch.

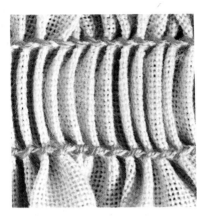

Outline

Worked similarly to ordinary stem stitch, each stitch picks up one pleat of the fabric. A firm control stitch, two rows worked at top or base of smocking will hold gathers firmly in place but it is not advisable to use this stitch at base of smocking where a loose flare is required (such as an angel top). Work from left to right.

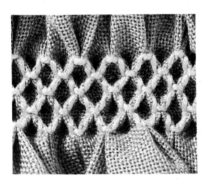

Vandyke

This is a small tight stitch worked from right to left. Bring needle through from back of work at second pleat from right. Then work a back stitch over the first two pleats. Go down to second row, take needle through second and third pleats and work a back stitch over them. Go back up to first row and work as before with third and fourth pleats. Continue across row in this way. Next row is worked similarly, starting on third row and working up to second. Simply thread needle behind previously worked back stitches of second row. Continue working in this way.

190

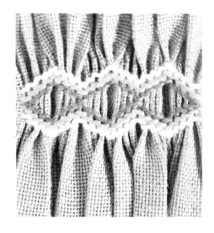

Wave stitch

Work from left to right in a similar way to cable stitch, in an upwards and downwards direction. While the upwards steps are being formed, the thread lies below the needle and when making the downward steps it lies above the needle. The second row is worked immediately below the first and so on. To create a diamond pattern as shown, work the next three rows with the zigzag lines going in the opposite direction.

Sorbello stitch

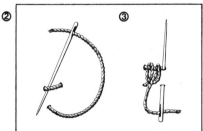

This is a knotted stitch which looks best worked in a thick yarn. Use it close together as a filling, in single rows or groups of rows as a border. Work from left to right, following steps 1 to 3 as illustrated.

Spanish, plaited

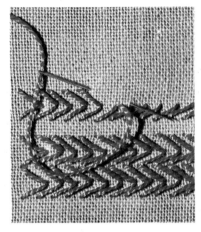

This is worked in two rows on counted threads, 5 along and 3 upwards with stitches converging in centre. Work first row from right to left, then turn work and travel from left to right, secure thread carefully because needle has to come up again where it went down.

Split stitch

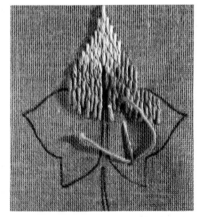

It looks rather like chain stitch and is ideal for outlining. It can be stitched in curving and spiral lines in close fillings as well as in straight lines. To work, make a short stitch then bring needle out again half way along it so that it pierces the working thread, split-

ting it into equal halves. Stitches can be gradually increased or decreased to fill a shape, but each should be brought up close to the centre of the previous one. Shorter stitches should be used on curves.

Stem stitch

This is rather like back stitch but is worked from left to right. Make a sloping stitch along the line of the design and then take needle back and bring it through again about half way along the previous stitch, on the lower side.

Stem band, raised

First work a line of parallel vertical stitches over area to be covered, then work lines of stem stitch over these threads without picking up fabric below.

S

191

S

The beautiful shapes and shades of peacock feathers have always been an inspiration to artists and designers. This example uses split stitch and stem stitch worked in stranded embroidery thread.

Straight lines, padded

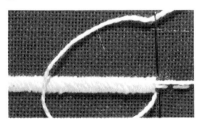

Add a new dimension and variety of texture by heightening the smooth flat surface of satin stitch with an underlayer of padding. To pad straight lines and stems, first cover line of the design with small running stitches. Then, cover these with a loose thread and stitch it to the fabric with small, close satin stitches. Cording is worked in a similar way, but with smaller stitches.

Surface darning

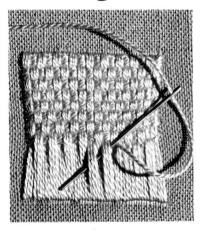

First make a foundation of closely worked satin stitch. Then, with either a matching or contrasting thread, weave over and under the foundation threads only in alternating groups of three threads. An open effect can be produced by slightly spacing the foundation threads.

Tatting

This is also known as shuttle lace or shuttle work. Shuttles are usually about 6.5cm (2½in) long and now made of plastic. The thread is tied to the centre of the shuttle for winding. Mercerized crochet cotton or linen thread can be used and a fine crochet hook is needed for joins.

Basic movements

Formation of half knot

Attach thread to centre of shuttle and wind it round until shuttle is full but without thread projecting beyond the edge. This ensures easy running. Leave about 50cm (20in) of thread hanging loose. Shuttle is always held in the right hand which is only used to supply the thread, all the tatting knots are formed with the left hand.

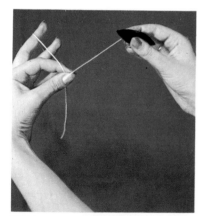

Hold thread on left, shuttle on right

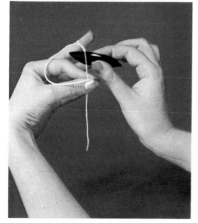

Pass shuttle from left to right

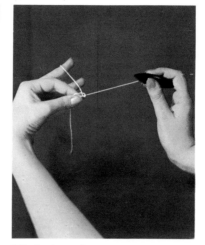

The basic tatting movement

(1) Hold end of thread between thumb and index finger of left hand and pass it over the other three fingers and back to form a large ring.

(2) Then lay thread from shuttle in a loose loop over top of left hand and pass shuttle from underneath upwards through both ring and loop from right to left.

(3) Next, for the basic tatting movement, lower middle finger of left hand to loosen the ring, then stretch shuttle thread horizontally to the right with right hand and pull it with a jerk. Then tighten up knot with left hand by raising middle finger again, so that knot slides on the shuttle thread. This last movement should be carried out perfectly without tightening knot too much so that this knot and all subsequent knots slide on the shuttle thread. As knots are made they should be held between index finger and thumb. Unwind thread from shuttle as it is needed.

The double knot (ds)

This is completed by the second half knot and is the basic tatting knot.

(1) The second half knot is worked in the opposite direction from the first. Wind thread round fingers of left hand again.

(2) Pass shuttle (held in right hand) from the top downwards through loop from left to right.

(3) The right hand holds the thread and keeps still while left hand closes up the second half knot. This completes the double knot which is then repeated.

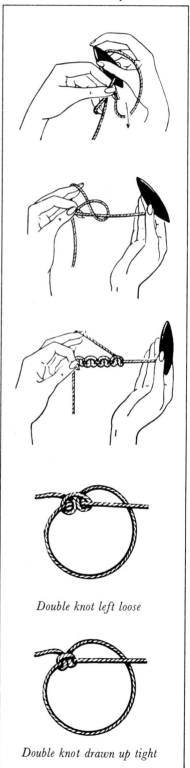

Double knot left loose

Double knot drawn up tight

T

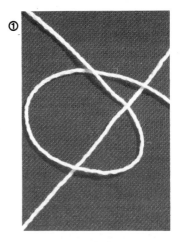

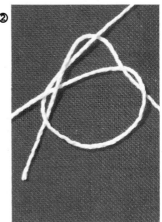

To join two ends of thread
Leave enough of the old thread to wind round hand and wind new thread round with old, to overlap. Work several knots with double thickness of thread, then drop old thread and continue with new. Cut away ends afterwards. Do not use double threads for picots. Illustrations show a weaver's knot. Use this method if you have made a mistake and have not been able to plan ahead for joining without a knot. However, ends can be knotted at beginning or end of a ring or chain and sewn in invisibly afterwards.
(1) Hold the two ends firmly crossed, left over right, with index finger and thumb of left hand. With right hand, pass the underneath thread over thumb of left hand to form a ring and through, between the two ends.
(2) Again with right hand, take end of other thread and insert it

downwards through the ring. Take the two ends and draw them upwards with right hand to tighten.

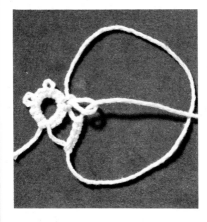

Joining rings (r)
Rings or pieces of tatting are joined together at a point where there is a picot. To do this, insert a small crochet hook through picot (see below) of previously made ring, draw through a loop of thread and catch it with the left fingers. Thread shuttle through this loop and draw up thread before beginning next knot. This joining knot is used in place of the first half of the double knot. The second half is then completed in the usual way.

Picots (p)
These are loops made by leaving free part of the thread between one knot and another.
(1) Make a double knot, leave a space of about 6mm ($\frac{1}{4}$in) and complete the next knot.

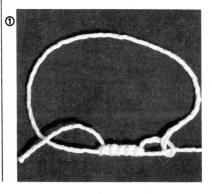

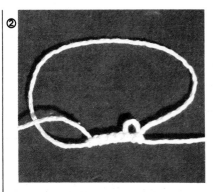

(2) Push the two knots together to make the loop before beginning the next knot.

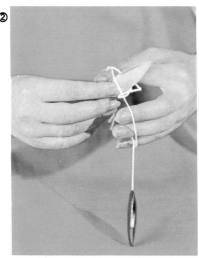

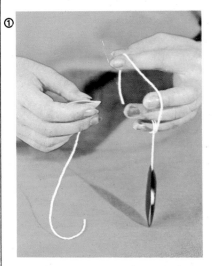

Working with two shuttles
The introduction of a second shuttle allows straight stitches to be added to rings or to link them in the form of chains. Chains are

194

worked with two threads, both on shuttles, it is helpful if shuttles are of different colours. Working with two shuttles also allows a different colour to be introduced to the work.

(1) Hold thread from left hand shuttle, gripping thread with thumb and index finger, winding it over middle and third finger and round little finger. The shuttle hangs loose.

(2) Take second shuttle in right hand and grip end of thread with thumb and index finger of left hand, together with first thread. Work double stitches in the usual way. Beginners will find it easier to tie these two threads together before working the knots. In this way the shuttle thread forms the stitch and the second shuttle carries the running thread. When changing from one to two shuttles, reverse the work. Usually, the shuttle used to make a ring is the shuttle which carries the running thread for the chain.

Motifs

Josephine knot
Make a series of 4 or 5 (or for a larger one, 10 or 12) half knots. Slip work off your hand and tighten shuttle thread to form a small ring. This knot is used as an ornament in various laces.

Ring and Josephine trimming on a napkin ring; instructions given overleaf

T

T

Ring trimming

Make 4 double knots, 1 picot, 4 doubles, 1 picot, 4 doubles, 1 picot, 4 doubles. Allow thread to feed in freely by stretching your fingers out and opening up the loop as required. Slip loop off fingers and draw up gently to close ring. Leave a space about 2.5cm (1in) long. To do this, wind thread around your left hand and adjust the length of the space as you make the next half knot. Anchor thread in position with left thumb. Complete 4 double knots, join to last picot of previous ring, then work second half of a double knot, work 3 doubles, 1 picot, 4 doubles, 1 picot, 4 doubles. Close ring. Make trimming as long as you need it and sew it on edge to be trimmed by the space threads between the rings. (For illustration, see Joining Rings).

Ring and Josephine trimming

This is a simple trimming which can be used to edge clothes, household linen, mats, tray cloths or lampshades.
Work a row of 5ds, 1p. 2ds, 1p, 2ds, 1p, 2ds, 1p, 5ds, close.
Reverse work by turning it up-side down. Leave a short space of thread (about 6mm ($\frac{1}{4}$in)) and work a Josephine knot consisting of the first half of a double knot worked 10 times. Reverse work again. Leave another thread space equal to the first and work a ring of 5ds, join to last picot of previous ring, then work 2ds, 1p, 2ds, 1p, 2ds, 1p, 2ds, 1p, 5ds, close.
Repeat from * to * as many times

as required to make length of edging needed. Remember to reverse work after each ring and after each Josephine knot, so that all the rings lie in one direction and all the Josephine knots in the opposite direction.

Teneriffe lace

This takes its name from the largest of the Canary Islands. It can be worked in squares, ovals, diamonds and straight borders, but the pattern most widely used is the circular star. Each star is made up separately and then sewn to the material or joined to other stars.
Materials needed are a compass, thin card, muslin or tracing paper, pencil, ruler, blunt ended tapestry needle, strong thread for support

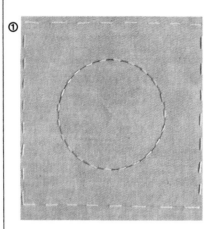

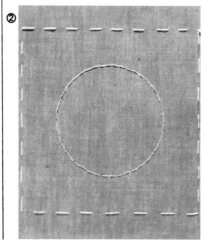

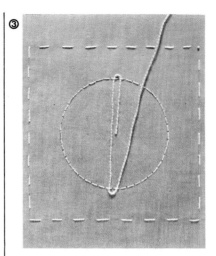

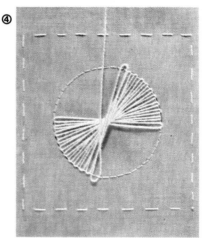

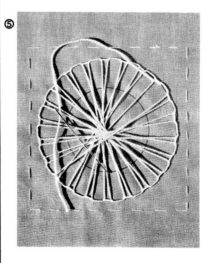

stitches (Coats satinized no.40), working thread (Coats mercer-crochet no.40, Clark's Anchor *coton à broder*, Clark's Anchor pearl).
It is simplest for a beginner to draw out the pattern in lines on

thin card forming the star shaped base on which designs are worked. Using a compass, draw a circle between 6.5 to 8cm (2½ to 3in) in diameter. With a ruler, divide circle in half, then quarters, and so on until you have 32 equally spaced segments. This is the simplest number to work with although this number can vary. Draw several concentric circles within the outline circle for the positioning of the decorative stitches. Place tracing paper or muslin over card and secure with tacking stitches forming an outside square (Basic pattern with segments not illustrated)

(1) Using strong thread, tack between the spokes, going across the edge of every alternate segment.

(2) Go round a second time to fill in the alternate segment previously missed.

(3) Make the spokes by starting at centre of circle with a knot on wrong side. This can be cut off afterwards, once last spoke has been worked and knotted to the first. Take yarn up through one support stitch, down through the one to the left of this and straight across to support stitch exactly opposite, down through this and up through stitch to the right.

(4) To make next spoke take thread up and through the left hand support stitch which has already been used, down through the support stitch to the left, across to right hand stitch which has already been used and back up through stitch to right of this. Continue until all the spokes have been worked. Finish off by taking thread to centre and knot it neatly to the beginning. Do not cut thread.

(5) Secure centre of star at crossing point with the same thread, working darning stitch over and under the spokes. Each time you complete a round and have returned to the point where you started weaving, take up two stitches together to maintain the alternated woven effect with previous row. Work as many rows as

Teneriffe lace can be worked directly from an illustration without a pattern or working instructions once the basic technique has been mastered. Contrasting colours and filling stitches add variety.

T

*Teneriffe lace mat has motifs applied round a fabric centre: each
motif consists of fifty petals held in place by circles of knotting.*

desired effect requires, taking care not to pull thread too tightly or you will draw in the star and distort the shape. Any joins in yarn must be as small as possible and neatest method is to use a weaver's knot (see Tatting). This is important as Teneriffe work is seen from both sides.

Motif with openwork centre

These are more practical for use as mats as the central section is flatter. Prepare pattern, drawing two concentric circles. If the inner circle is a great deal smaller than the outer one, the number of spaces to work will differ so this number must be calculated carefully. It should be either two fifths or one quarter of the outer circle. Work running stitches over the two circles as before. Work out length of thread needed to make the spokes and knot thread on wrong side.

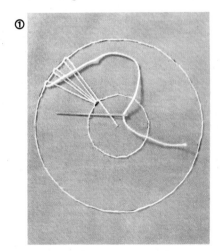

(1) Take yarn under a support stitch in inner circle and under corresponding stitch in outer circle. Take yarn under next support stitch of outer circle and return to inner circle, again taking yarn under first support stitch. Continue, working only once under each stitch of outer circle but two or three times under each stitch of inner circle. Work in this way if inner circle is two fifths of outer one.

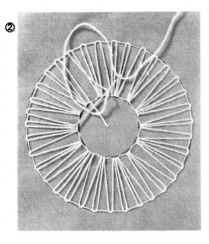

(2) If inner circle is one quarter of outer one, thread must be taken four times under each stitch of inner circle and once under each stitch of outer circle. When all spokes have been made, fasten off thread at starting point.

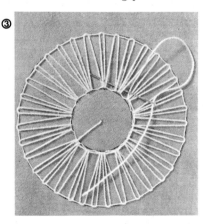

(3) Work running stitch round centre, over and under alternate threads. Secure thread by knotting it to starting thread.

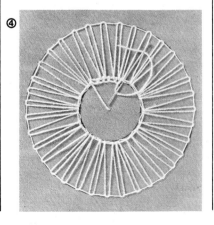

(4) Work a row of buttonhole stitches around inner circle, making one stitch between every two spokes.

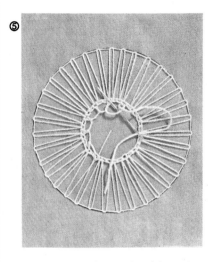

(5) Next, work a twisted loop between every three buttonhole stitches, leaving thread loose as shown.

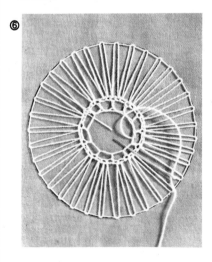

(6) Overcast over loops, then work a final row of buttonhole stitch, making one stitch for every three of the preceding row.

Border

To make pattern draw two parallel lines, making their distance apart the required width of band. Work running stitches along these parallel lines as for circular motif. The bars of the lace will be worked between these lines. Bars

199

T

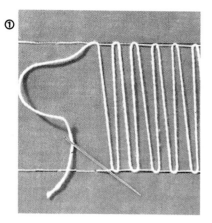

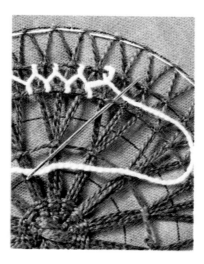

Transferring designs

can be worked in two different ways (1) in a zigzag when stitches worked will alternate and (2) criss-crossed when stitches worked will be parallel.

Decorating motifs

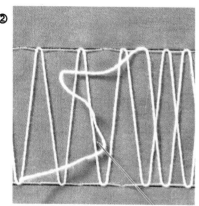

Knotting
Two or more threads can be grouped as illustrated, knotting them together with a twisted chain stitch.

Open Cretan stitch
Work two parallel rows of knotting then loop a contrasting thread up and down between the rows, always keeping thread on the right and making stitches as shown.

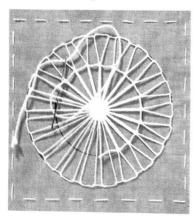

Twisted threads
This technique is also used in drawn thread work with running stitch, twisting threads as you work. Needle is slipped under second thread, twisted back and brought out eye first ready for the next twist so that spokes are twisted over each other as shown.

Finishing off
Cut support stitches to free star from card, join to subsequent stars or insert into fabric.

With carbon paper
Yellow or light blue carbon paper can be used on dark fabrics, black or dark blue on light. Place carbon paper face downwards on fabric, then place drawing or tracing of design to be used on top. Draw over lines of design with a sharp pointed pencil. Take care to press only on lines of the design or carbon is liable to smudge the fabric.

Ironing on transfer
Specially prepared transfers can be ironed directly on to the fabric. There are two types: single impression and multiprint which gives up to eight impressions

Transfers, yarns and inspiration. Ferns come in all sorts of lovely shapes

Parsley Fern (p. 30).
Cryptogramme crispa.

T

depending on weight of fabric being used (more impressions can be made on a finer fabric). Work on a flat surface. Establish centre of transfer by folding it in half twice, then find centre of chosen position for design in the same way. Match centre of transfer with this point. For single impression transfers, cut off any waste lettering from transfer. Heat iron to wool setting and test transfer on a corner or scrap of cloth by placing spare lettering face downwards and applying iron for a few seconds. If transfer takes, you can begin to transfer design itself. Place it face downwards on fabric and pin each corner. Protect fabric not covered by transfer with tissue paper. Apply iron for a few seconds and remove. Lift one corner carefully to see if transfer has taken. If not, re-iron gently, making sure you have not moved transfer or fabric as this will give a double impression. Use multiprint transfers similarly but with the iron on cotton setting. If transfer does not take the first time, allow it to cool before re-ironing.

Tracing (pouncing)
This is a very old method of transferring designs on to fabric. If equipment shown in illustration is not available it can be easily improvised. Materials required are a dabber which can be made of a wad of felt or a pad of wad-ding, a fine brush for painting in the outlines of the design, a pad of blanket or felt on which to prick the tracing paper, a large darning needle or pin to prick out the design, tracing paper, water colour paint in a dark or light colour to contrast with fabric being used, powdered charcoal (for light coloured fabrics) and powdered chalk (for dark fabrics). Trace design required on to tracing paper and place this right side down on the blanket pad, then with needle prick small holes along all the lines of the design, spacing them evenly about 2mm ($\frac{1}{16}$in) apart. Place pricked design on to fabric and secure in position with weights.

Rub powdered charcoal or chalk through pricked holes using dabber and plenty of powder. When whole design has been covered, remove tracing paper carefully. Design should now be clearly defined in a series of dots. Blow off surplus powder and paint over dotted lines with water colour paint.

If working with a fine fabric which is also transparent such as organdie, fine silk or nylon, design can be traced directly on to fabric by placing design underneath and painting over lines with water colour paint or tracing with soft pencil.

If working on coarse or textured fabric where pile makes it difficult to trace or paint a design, trace drawing on to tracing paper, tack paper in position on fabric and carefully mark off lines of design with running stitches. Tear tracing away before beginning to embroider and remove tacking stitches after work is completed.

Tucks

Cross
These tucks are made before fabric is cut out. Working on right side, carefully mark width of tucks and spaces between them (a cardboard gauge is useful for

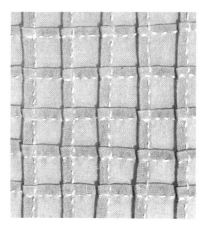

this). Fabric should be creased along a horizontal thread so that each tuck is on the true grain. Stitch by hand or machine, working horizontal tucks first and then pressing them all in the same direction. When making the vertical lines, tack each intersection carefully to prevent tucks slipping.

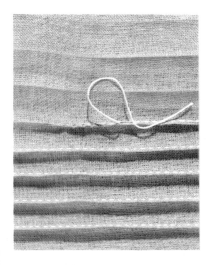

Pin
These are very fine tucks and must be evenly spaced. Use a cardboard gauge as for cross tucks working very carefully on the grain of the fabric before fabric is cut out. Tucks should be no wider than a pin head, they make an effective surface decoration when used on a flat textured, fairly thin fabric.

Enchanting christening robe and bonnet exquisitely tucked and lace trimmed

T

Tunisian crochet

Tunisian crochet draws on the techniques of both crochet and knitting.

It produces strong, thick fabrics which are ideal for sportswear and heavier garments although lighter fabrics can also be achieved. The fabric is produced with a special Tunisian crochet hook which looks like a knitting needle with a hook at the end instead of a point. These are available in one length but a large range of sizes. Tunisian crochet takes from crochet the basic principle of beginning with a chain, but then one loop from each stitch is lifted onto the hook as you work along the length of starting chain, from right to left. A second row completes the pattern, this is worked from left to right without turning work round and reduces the number of loops until only one remains.

Classic Tunisian stitch

Begin with a chain consisting of an even number of stitches.

Foundation row (1) Insert hook into 2nd ch from hook, put yarn round hook — called yrh —, and draw one loop through ch, * insert hook into next ch, yrh and draw through one loop, rep from * to end. Number of loops on hook should now be the same as the number of chain worked at beginning.

2nd row (2) Do not turn work, yrh, and draw loop through first loop on hook, * yrh and draw through 2 loops on hook, rep from * until one loop remains. This is working from left to right hand edge.

3rd row (3) 1ch, * insert hook from right to left through first upright thread of previous row, yrh and draw through one loop, rep from * into every upright thread working along the row to the left. Once again, number of loops on

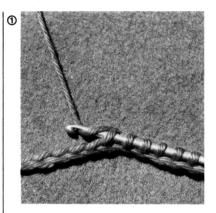

hook should be the same as number of chain worked at beginning.

4th row As 2nd.

The 3rd and 4th rows are repeated for the required length (4). Always finish with a 2nd row and for a neat finish work 1 row double crochet into the last row of upright threads.

Because of the way in which Tunisian crochet is worked, it has a tendency to twist sideways. This can be corrected when finished work is pressed, but can be lessened by not making fabric too tight. It will be tighter if the 'yrh' is not pulled adequately through the stitch so that only a tiny loop is formed and also if yarn is held too tightly or if too fine a hook is used. When starting to work towards the right never pull first stitch so tightly that you flatten or pull down the height of the row.

Fabric stitches

Check stitch

Work in classic Tunisian stitch, working 3 sts in each colour and alternating the colours on every 4th row.

Strand the yarn not in use loosely behind the work.

Cluster

This stitch can be varied to suit the purpose for which it is required. It is worked on a ground of classic Tunisian stitch, working the clusters where required by

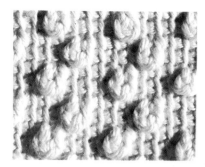

making 4 or 5 chain before continuing the next stitch. The chain or cluster formed should be left on the right side of the work. Use cluster stitch distributed evenly on the fabric as an all-over pattern or grouped together in geometric areas.

Crossed
Worked over an even number of chain

Foundation row As given for classic Tunisian stitch.

2nd row As 2nd row of classic Tunisian stitch.

3rd row 1ch, * insert hook into 3rd upright thread of previous row, yrh and draw through one loop, insert hook into 2nd upright thread and draw through one loop, rep from * to end, working into 5th then 4th, 7th then 6th upright threads etc.

4th row As 2nd.

5th and 6th rows As classic Tunisian stitch.

7th row As 3rd.

8th row As 4th.

The 5th to 8th rows are repeated for the required length.

Neat little Tunisian crochet waistcoat with a tapestry effect.

T

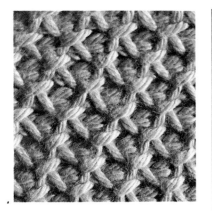

Cross-over stitch
1st and 2nd rows In classic Tunisian stitch.

3rd row 1ch, * yrh twice, taking the yarn from front to back, insert hook behind the next 2 vertical loops, rep from * to end, pick up 1 loop in the last st.

4th row Work the loops off in the usual way.

5th row As 3rd row but alternating the pairs of stitches.

The 2nd to 5th rows form the pattern.

Fence stitch
Make a foundation chain the required length.

1st row * Yrh, insert hook into next ch and draw up a loop, yrh and draw through 2 loops on hook, rep from * to end.

2nd row Work off the loops in pairs in the usual way.

3rd row as 1st row, but inserting hook behind the vertical loop of stitches.

Repeat the 2nd and 3rd rows as required.

Knot stitch
This is worked on a background of classic Tunisian stitch.

Work the first row in the ordinary way. On the return row, work to the place where the knot is required, work 5ch, insert hook into the first of these 5ch, yrh, and draw through 3 loops on hook (i.e. the 1st ch, the working loop on hook and the next st along the row).

Mahogany stitch
Make a foundation ch the required length.

Work 2 rows in classic Tunisian stitch.

3rd row 1ch, * insert hook behind vertical loop of next st and draw up a loop, yrh, insert the hook again behind the same st and draw up a loop, yrh and draw through 3 loops on hook, rep from * to end, working into the last loop in the usual way (1).

4th row Work the sts off in the usual way.

Rep the 3rd and 4th rows for length required. (2).

Rib
Worked over an even number of chain.

1st and 2nd rows As given for classic Tunisian stitch.

3rd row 1ch, * insert hook into 3rd upright thread of previous row, yrh and draw through one loop, insert hook into 2nd upright thread, yrh and draw through one loop, continue from * in this way working in groups of 2 and crossing the threads by working the 5th then 4th, 7th then 6th etc, ending with one st in last upright thread.

4th row As classic Tunisian stitch. Repeat 3rd and 4th rows as required. If pattern is worked over stitches which are being decreased or increased, care must be taken to see that the crossed stitches come immediately above the crossed stitches of the previous row, or ribbed effect will be spoilt.

It is important to draw through a loop that is fairly loose on the hook, otherwise work will be very close and thick.

Rib (diagonal)

Worked over an even number of chain.

1st and 2nd rows Work as given for classic Tunisian stitch.

3rd and 4th rows Work as given for rib stitch.

5th row 1ch, work into next up-right thread, yrh and draw loop through, then work one stitch into each of next 2 stitches, working the furthest away first then returning to work the missed one, rep to end of row.

6th row As given for 2nd row of classic Tunisian stitch.

Repeat 3rd to 6th rows as required.

Star stitch

Make a foundation ch having a multiple of 3 sts and 2 extra sts. Work 2 rows in classic Tunisian stitch.

3rd row 1ch, * insert hook behind the next 3 vertical loops, yrh and draw up a loop, 1ch, insert hook

into the space made be the 1ch and draw up a loop, insert hook into the sp after the 3 sts which were worked tog and draw up a loop, rep from * to end, draw up 1 loop in last st,

4th row Work the loops off in the usual way.

The 3rd and 4th rows form the pattern.

Stocking stitch

Worked over an even number of chain.

Foundation row. As given for classic Tunisian stitch.

2nd row As 2nd row of classic Tunisian stitch.

3rd row 1ch, * insert hook from front to back *between* upright threads of previous row, yrh and draw through one loop, rep from * to end.

4th row As 2nd.

The 3rd and 4th rows are repeated for the required length.

Treble

Worked over an even number of chain.

Foundation row. Yrh, insert hook into 3rd ch from hook, yrh and draw through ch, yrh and draw through 2 loops, * yrh, insert hook into next ch, yrh and draw through 2 loops, rep from * to end.

2nd row As 2nd row of classic Tunisian stitch.

3rd row 2ch, * yrh and insert hook from right to left into upright thread of previous row, yrh and draw through one loop, yrh and draw through 2 loops, rep from * to end.

4th row As 2nd row of classic Tunisian stitch.

The 3rd and 4th rows are repeated for the required length.

T

Openwork stitches

Eyelet
Worked over an even number of chain.

Foundation row Yrh twice, insert hook into 3rd ch from hook, yrh and draw through one loop, yrh and draw through 2 loops, * yrh twice, insert hook into next ch, yrh and draw through one loop, yrh and draw through 2 loops, rep from * to end.

2nd row As 2nd row classic Tunisian stitch.

3rd row 2ch, * yrh twice, insert hook into upright thread *and* slightly sloping upright thread to right of it made in previous row, yrh and draw through one loop, yrh and draw through 2 loops, rep from * to end.

4th row As 2nd.

The 3rd and 4th rows are repeated for the required length.

Fan stitch
Make a foundation ch the required length, having a multiple

of 3 sts plus 1 extra. Work 3 rows in classic Tunisian stitch

4th row (return row) yrh and draw through first loop, * 2ch, yrh and draw through the loop on hook and the next 3 loops, rep from * to end. (1)

5th row 1ch, * insert hook into each of next 2ch and draw up a loop, insert hook into the vertical loops of the 3 sts which were worked tog and draw up a loop, rep from * to end, working into the last 2ch, then into the vertical loop of the end st.

6th row Work the sts off in pairs in the usual way.

The 3rd to 6th rows form the pattern. (2)

Four-sided stitch
Make a foundation chain the required length, having an even number of ch.

1st row *Yrh, miss 1ch, insert hook into next ch and draw up a loop, rep from * to end.

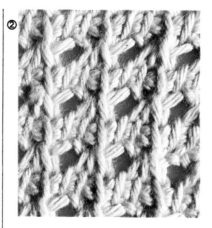

2nd row Work off the loops in pairs in the usual way.

3rd row As 1st row, but inserting hook behind the vertical loop of stitches.

Rep the 2nd and 3rd rows as required.

Buttonholes

Mark position for buttonhole with pins on right side of work before beginning right side row. Work to beginning of marked position. Wind yarn round hook for the number of stitches over which the hole must stretch, miss this number of stitches and continue to end of row. On the next row work off each loop of yarn as if it were one stitch.

Decreasing

To decrease one stitch at right hand edge as illustrated insert hook through 2 upright threads, yrh

208

and draw through only one loop, working to end of row in normal way. To decrease one stitch at end of row, work in same way by inserting hook through the last 2 upright threads together, yrh and draw through only one loop.

Increasing

At beginning of row
(1) To increase one stitch at beginning of a right side row, or the right hand edge of work, work 1 chain then insert hook under the horizontal thread between the first and second upright threads, yrh and draw through one loop. Continue working into next and following upright threads in normal way.

At end of row
(2) Work in same way by inserting hook under the horizontal thread between the second to last and last stitches, yrh and draw through one loop. Work the last stitch in usual way.

Two or more stitches at beginning of row
(1) To increase more than one stitch at beginning of a row, work that number of chain. Into the chain work classic Tunisian stitch and continue along the row.

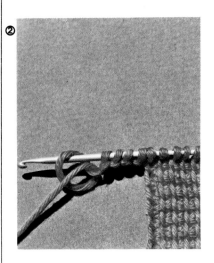

Two or more stitches at end of row
(2) At the left hand end of a right side row, put on to the hook the required number of slip stitches. Continue to work next row in usual way.

Shapes

Diamond
Make 2ch and work the first 2 rows (forward and return) in the usual way.

3rd row 1ch, insert hook into first upright loop (edge st) and draw up a loop, insert hook into next loop and draw up a loop (3 loops now on hook, 1 st has been increased at the beg on row).

4th row Make 2ch, then work off the loops in the usual way. (1 st has now been increased at end of row.)

5th row 1ch, insert hook into the first upright loop (edge st) and draw up a loop, draw up a loop in every stitch to end, insert hook into the 1ch before the end loop and draw up a loop. Then insert hook into the end loop and draw up a loop.

6th row Make 2ch, then work off all loops in the usual way.

Repeat the 5th and 6th rows until there is the required number of stitches.

To decrease, on the outward row, insert the hook into the last 2 loops of the row together and draw up a loop, on the return row work the last 3 loops tog.

T

Triangle
This is worked in the same way as the first half of the diamond. Cast off in the usual way.

Tunisian braid
Make 5ch.
1st row Miss first 1ch, *insert hook into next ch yrh and draw up a loop, rep from * 3 times more, keeping all the loops on hook (you now have 5 loops) yrh and draw through first loop, (yrh and draw through next 2 loops) 4 times.
2nd row * Insert hook into vertical thread of next st, yrh and draw up a loop, rep from * 3 times more (you now have 5 loops on hook). Complete as for 1st

row. Rep 2nd row for length required.

Turkish, triangular

This reversible stitch gives the effect of a drawn fabric stitch. It is worked on counted threads, five across and five upwards in diagonal stages to and fro, the double diagonal lines being formed on the return journey.

Turkish embroidery

This work is now carried out in brightly coloured yarns on natural canvas although originally it was worked in gold thread on scarlet or violet velvet. Turkish stitch is combined with cross stitch, satin, long and short and chain stitch. Variations of Turkish stitch can be used for filling, applying lace or fabric.

Turkish stitch

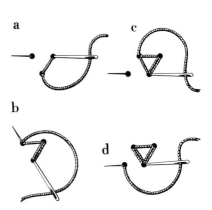

a   c

b   d

This is used for appliqué. Work from right to left, following diagrams, each part of the stitch will be double. Pick up three or more threads of background fabric and three or more threads of fabric being applied, which has previously been tacked into position. When first triangular stitch has been completed, take needle out six threads or more along to the left and repeat.

Turkish, squared

Another decorative stitch which resembles hem stitching and can

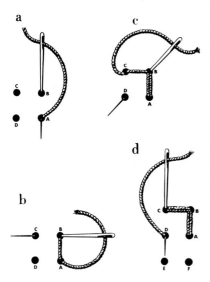

also be used for applying one fabric to another, each part of stitch will be double. Work from right to left following diagrams. Pick up two or more threads of fabric being applied and two or more threads of background fabric. For next stitch, take needle out four or more threads to the left and repeat.

Turning triangle

Work one row upwards, one row downwards. Take thread diagonally across five threads and horizontally across five threads, making a back stitch.

Turning triangles make an attractive filling. Other stitches add variety.

U-Z

Under-stitching

This is used on neck or armhole facings after they have been stitched to a garment and prevents facings rolling outwards. On wrong side, press both seam allowances towards facing and stitch on right side of facing, just outside seam line, through all thicknesses of seam allowances and facing. Turn facing to inside of garment, press in position and lightly sew facing edges to seam allowances only.

Velvet, embroidery on

This is extremely difficult to work. Satin stitch is embroidered over foundation shapes cut out in thin cardboard and lightly glued in position with fabric adhesive. Work should be held in a frame.

Waistbands

Cut fabric for band to waist measurement plus about 3.5cm (1¼in) overlap by double width required, add seam allowances all round. For stiffening cut a length of petersham to exact size of finished waistband. Lightly catch petersham to wrong side of front half of band. Pin band to skirt, right sides together, raw edges level and stitch along seam line. Press seam towards band. Fold band in half, turn under free edge and tack to skirt so that it covers stitching line. Slip stitch in place, also turning in and stitching ends of overlap. Stitch on hooks and eyes to fasten, overlapping front over back.

X marks the spot

Pinpoint the position for a button or a press stud by criss crossing two pins so that the intersection marks the exact spot for the fastening. Bring needle through at this point when beginning to sew.

Yugoslav embroidery

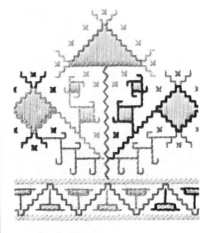

Geometric designs are generally used for this work. Popular stitches are satin, stem, buttonhole, double back and cross stitch more often embroidered in wool than in cotton on coarsely woven fabric.

Zip fasteners

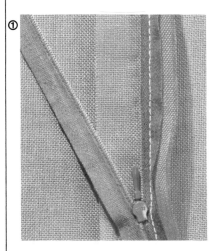

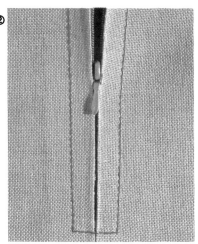

Prepare opening on garment by tacking seams together along the seam line. Press open carefully. Remove tacking. Open zip fastener to bottom and lay it in opening so that seam edges just cover the zip teeth on both sides. Tack the zip into position (1). To check that seams lie perfectly flat, close the zip before finally machine stitching it into position. Start stitching about 1cm (⅜in) down from seam edge on one side, stitch down until level with end of the zip. Turn work and stitch across seam. Pivot work on needle and stitch up other side. Remove tacking and press lightly on wrong side avoiding teeth of nylon zip fastener. (Use a special zip foot for machine stitching).

Index